MANAGING CAPITAL
BUDGET PROJECTS

THE WILEY/RONALD SERIES IN PROFESSIONAL ACCOUNTING AND BUSINESS

Lee J. Seidler, Series Editor

Managing Capital Budget Projects

A PREEMPTIVE AUDIT APPROACH

FELIX POMERANZ, C.P.A.
Partner, Coopers & Lybrand

A RONALD PRESS PUBLICATION
JOHN WILEY & SONS
New York • Chichester • Brisbane • Toronto • Singapore

This publication is designed to provide accurate and
authoritative information in regard to the subject
matter covered. It is sold with the understanding that
the publisher is not engaged in rendering legal, accounting,
or other professional service. If legal advice or other
expert assistance is required, the services of a competent
professional person should be sought. *From a Declaration
of Principles jointly adopted by a Committee of the
American Bar Association and a Committee of Publishers.*

Library of Congress Cataloging in Publication Data:

Pomeranz, Felix.
    Managing capital budget projects.

    (The Wiley/Ronald series in professional accounting
and business)
    "A Ronald Press publication."
    Bibliography: p.
    Includes index.
    1. Auditing   2. Capital Investments—Accounting.
3. Capital budget—Accounting.   I. Title.   II. Series

HF 5667.P593   1984   658.1'54   83-2656
ISBN 0-471-09799-3

Printed in the United States of America

10 9 8 7 6 5 4 3 2

Preface

A former senior partner of the international firm of Coopers & Lybrand recently wrote: "Within its field of learning, a profession has a responsibility to give leadership to the community which it serves. This is provided by research, experiment and innovation, constantly improving methods and techniques, and better organization. It must therefore plan to keep abreast of, and preferably just ahead of, public thought and opinion."*

The Preemptive Auditing® approach is my endeavor to make meaningful—from a management perspective—the technological and behavioral knowledge that is part of today's auditor's tool kit. And, importantly, I consider an "auditor" not a stereotype but that concerned "hearer" who listens to managers at all levels—not with a view toward ex post facto comments, but as an activist in improving operations.

Preemptive Auditing is in its infancy. The possibilities open to a Preemptive Auditor who is desirous of helping to enhance revenues or contain costs are limited only by the solidity of the auditor's accomplishments and by imagination. Throughout the book we have used a gray screen to highlight points perceived to be of the greatest interest to the reader.

I would be remiss if I did not acknowledge professional indebtedness to teachers, associates, and clients who imbued me with an ideal of constantly seeking to improve professional practice. The seminal writings of Elmer Staats, retired Comptroller General of the United States, deserve mention.

The firm of Coopers & Lybrand, and particularly its Chairman, Peter R. Scanlon, and its Vice Chairman, Charles F. Jacey, must be commended for cooperation and support. The firm's Preemptive Auditing Group, composed

*Benson, Lord Henry, "The Professions and the Community" in Statements in Quotes, *Journal of Accountancy*, April 1983, pp. 90–103.

of partners Robert M. Bird, Evandro F. Braz, Frederick J. Koczwara, and Philip J. Schulz, was generous in sharing its views and expertise; particular mention is due to two members of the staff, Thomas F. Ochab, P.E., and Eugene D. Yano, C.P.A., who read various`drafts of this work and offered perceptive comments.

Most importantly, I would like to acknowledge my debt to client executives who voiced confidence in the Preemptive Audit concept and helped to see the vision into practice: John M. Butler, William Cavanaugh III, John C Pickett, and Edward V. Regan.

FELIX POMERANZ

New York, New York
January, 1984

Contents

MANAGING CAPITAL
BUDGET PROJECTS

PART ONE

Concepts

CHAPTER ONE

Introduction

Nineteen hundred years ago, during the reign of the Emperor Claudius, the Romans completed the modernization of the port of Ostia, which served their capital city. According to contemporary sources, the project required 100 years from visualization to completion and the cost exceeded the original estimate by about 25 percent, even though that estimate was based on a more ambitious plan than was ultimately adopted. The fact that the ancients recorded this cost overrun indicates that they regarded it as at least noteworthy. We must agree with this assessment, but not for the same reasons. The Romans thought the figure was high; to us it is astonishingly low. Today we accept as a fact of life overruns of 50 percent or more. In the early 1970s, the U.S. General Accounting Office found in a survey that actual costs of large government projects exceeded budgeted costs by an *average* of 50 percent!

Recently an approach has been developed that enables management to improve, often drastically, its control over cost, quality, and timeliness, especially in capital investments. The approach, known as Preemptive Auditing (from the Latin *prae* meaning "before," plus *emere*—"to buy"), or less commonly, preemptive systems review or technical planning review, involves evaluation of business actions or decisions *before* the actions are completed or the decisions implemented—for example, while contracts are executory or budgets are being drawn up.

The new approach represents a fundamental conceptual departure from conventional auditing, which may detect faulty practices but often not until after their effects have been felt.

Functional Characteristics of the Preemptive Audit

The Preemptive Audit is carried out within a framework similar to the conventional audit, but there are fundamental differences in timing and coverage between the new and the traditional audit concepts. The Preemptive Audit focuses on *all* control practices helpful to management, and utilizes *all* information that can be expressed in numbers and verified; in no sense is the Preemptive Audit restricted to accounting or financial matters.

Preemptive Auditing has certain features in common with consulting—direct observation of activities and a high degree of concern with the performance of client personnel, for example—but the two techniques cannot be equated. A major difference lies in their characteristic response to findings of deficiency; in Preemptive Auditing corrective action is implemented immediately.

Applications

The Preemptive Audit technique can be applied to all plans and programs in either the private or public sectors that are relatively discrete, subject to planning, managed by designated individuals, subject to measurement, and prone to control and accounting. Examples of potential applications include capital investment, cash management, marketing research, procurement, traffic management, and personnel management. Although applications are as broad as the imaginations of users, in the current economic climate interest is likely to focus on control of construction costs and related capital investment management aspects.

Benefits

The most important improvements that management can anticipate as a result of Preemptive Auditing are those affecting:

Project performance, in terms of adherence to budget, schedule, and quality targets.

Credibility with regulatory bodies, lenders, and contractors, and with its own personnel.

Economy, in terms of hard-core savings resulting from the application of preferred practices to operations.

Because the Preemptive Audit serves primarily to prevent loss, its benefits are difficult to measure. It is possible, however, to estimate exposure to risk by deriving a factor for the amount of the potential loss and a factor for the probability of that loss and multiplying one by the other.

Background

The possibility of using an audit-type approach for the planning and management of capital investments has been recognized for some time. It wasn't until after World War II, however, when electronic data processing (EDP) revolutionized recordkeeping and made possible the application of mathematically based models to aid in the decision-making process, that the implementation of the preaudit concept began to receive serious consideration.

Among the first to appreciate the implications of the new approach was Elmer Staats, former Comptroller General of the United States. In an article published in *GAO Review* some years ago, Mr. Staats declared: "Traditionally, auditors like to look at records of transactions that occurred weeks or months ago and check on the way they were handled, to reach a conclusion as to whether such transactions were proper, economical, and so on. The days in which such auditing can be done are numbered. . . . In the systems of the future we will have to audit transactions as they occur before there is necessarily a record to look at. This will mean that much better audit planning will be needed, so that many tasks now performed sequentially can be performed more or less simultaneously. Without far greater planning than is now given most audits, such audits can not be done."[*]

In recent years, the fulfillment of Mr. Staats' prediction has been favored by a decline in the cost of computer hardware and peripherals which aid Preemptive Auditing.

In 1978 the first known instance of a formal engagement to perform a Preemptive Audit occurred when the Arkansas Power and Light Company (AP&L) received permission from the state's public service commission to construct a steam electric station. Approval for the $800 million project was contingent upon the "appointment of independent public accountants, responsible to the Commission, who would: (a) monitor the construction of the plant; (b) review all contracts entered into in connection with construction of

---

[*]Elmer B. Staats, "The Increasing Importance of Internal Auditors in Today's World," *GAO Review*, Fall 1977, pp. 1–8.

the plant; (c) submit semiannual reports to the Commission identifying deviations from budgeted construction expenditures and the reasonableness of deviations. . . ." Pursuant to that order the utility appointed the author's firm to perform the tasks mentioned. Much of the credit for this important event belongs to Dr. John Pickett, then the Arkansas Public Service Commission's (APSC) chairman, at whose behest the Commission acted.

The First Five Years

In the few cases so far, in which a complete Preemptive Audit has been carried out, results have been encouraging. Recently AP&L's Independence steam electric station underwent a complete, independently conducted examination directed at project controls. The examiners, a firm of consulting engineers with high visibility in the utility field, declared that they had seen no better managed project in the United States. The same Preemptive Audit produced a saving of $20 million on a general plant contract of $150 million by demonstrating the cost advantage of a lump-sum over a cost-plus arrangement.

Elements of the Preemptive Audit—An Overview

Rudyard Kipling once wrote that he had "five serving men tried and true, their names were what, when, how, why, and who." Kipling's investigative method has been used in the following survey of Preemptive Auditing.

What

The Preemptive Audit comprises a series of procedural exercises each grouped under a designated objective. The full audit for a construction project comprises achievement of 23 objectives (see Appendix I) and of the related tasks; however, in given circumstances a lesser number of effort areas may be sufficient, depending upon the complexity of the project, its duration, and its specific needs. In general, the scope of the Preemptive Audit is determined by management even if the audit is performed by outside parties.

Broadly construed, the "what" heading also includes a number of steps that are not a part of the audit but which in most cases should be performed as a preliminary to it. (For government and not-for-profit entities, the steps should be regarded as virtually mandatory.) These steps are as follows:

1. Formulation of program objectives:
    (a) In terms specific enough to provide a sound basis for assessing results.
    (b) With full regard for the views of all who will exercise major responsibilities in the construction project or other activity to be audited.
2. Formulation of techniques for achieving the objectives, on the basis of agreement between all the concerned parties within the organization.
3. Communication of the objectives, together with the agreed-on techniques for their accomplishment, to all whose views were considered in formulating the objectives and techniques.
4. Assignment of responsibilities for controlling the activity to be audited and for monitoring its progress, to designated persons provided with the necessary resources.

When

We would say as soon as possible. The later a Preemptive Audit is started, the less the prospect of a beneficial impact on cost, timing, and quality.

How

The Preemptive Audit is carried out by following a syllabus of procedures designed to test for deficiencies, that is to identify departures from preferred practices, and to correct them. These procedures are described in detail in the how-to section which comprises the bulk of this book.

Why

The rationale for Preemptive Auditing is of course implied in almost all of the foregoing discussion. If that rationale could be expressed in one trenchant phrase, it would be that of the executive who spoke of "protecting one's derrière."

Who

Preemptive Auditing is designed to be applicable by upper and middle management. Thus the party in charge of the Preemptive Audit may hold the position of company president, chief engineering officer, vice-president for finance, or member of the board of directors, as well as construction manager, internal auditor, or manager in the engineering department.

The Preemptive Audit manager will normally delegate at least some of the specific duties associated with the audit to the appropriate persons. For planning, engineering, and design aspects, these assistants will probably be senior technical people. For monitoring of performance and testing of controls they may be junior personnel trained in accounting and auditing. The choice of specific persons will depend on in-house capabilities. Where persons who combine the requisite knowledge with available time are lacking, recourse to independent auditors or consultants is the logical step.

Organizations that have several activities underway at one time, state agencies in particular, may find it useful to set up a permanent Preemptive Audit capability to handle all their Preemptive Audit needs. (At least one state has been exploring the possibility of creating a permanent team to service projects under state jurisdiction.) For this purpose, an important role is foreseen for independent auditors or consultants. (Admittedly there are as yet few independent practitioners prepared to carry out this task.)

The Plan of the Book

The book contains a conceptual and implementational section. The conceptual section (Chapters 1 to 5) discusses the nature and objectives of Preemptive Auditing. It explains general techniques as well as specialized techniques, such as a review of budgeting.

Chapters 6 to 10 spell out planning issues, objectives and techniques likely to contribute to achievement of those objectives, together with the review routines to be applied by the Preemptive Auditor. The coverage in Chapters 11 to 17 is primarily concerned with compliance, that is with offering a measure of assurance that the controls intended to have been instituted are functioning as planned. Wherever possible, sources of supplementary information are indicated and how-to instructions provided.

CHAPTER TWO

The Nature
of the Preemptive Audit

The traditional (financial) audit may be defined as directed toward the expression of an opinion, certifying that financial statements have been prepared in accordance with generally accepted accounting principles. This type of audit is conducted pursuant to generally accepted auditing standards, prescribed in the professional liturgy.

Although the basic stages that go to make the conventional audit are defined in various ways, there is general agreement as to their nature. The author's firm recognizes six, as follows:

Obtaining an understanding of the business, system, and operations.

Recording that understanding, generally by means of flow charts.

Testing certain controls to ensure that they are in place and functioning as planned.

Evaluating control deficiencies in relation to the program for "substantive" tests, those tests largely designed to verify account balances.

Preparing a letter to management.

Performing substantive tests and other audit procedures necessary to the expression of the opinion.

The Preemptive Audit and the Financial Audit Compared

To some extent the foregoing steps are present in a Preemptive Audit, with significant differences.

In obtaining an understanding there is little difference between the financial and the Preemptive Audit, with one exception. In a Preemptive Audit, emphasis is placed on evaluation of *owner* risk; the Preemptive Auditor is required to understand the environment in which the business operates and the potential losses to which it may be exposed. After causes of loss have been identified, a dollar value may be assigned to the exposure, enabling the Preemptive Auditor to determine whether the risk should be disregarded, assumed, shifted to others, or managed, possibly via a mix of techniques. In addition, the audit should enable him or her to recommend the resources to be assigned to management of the risk.

With respect to the recording of the understanding, financial auditing demands considerable detail in keeping with the auditor's need to identify controls upon which he or she may eventually rely in terms of restricting his or her substantive tests. (Substantive tests may be limited, or their timing shifted, if the auditor's tests of compliance have established that controls are in effect and functioning as planned.) In a Preemptive Audit, on the other hand, flow charts are likely to show less detail and more overview information; specific descriptions of processing, files, and reports are likely to be minimal.

With regard to testing of controls, important conceptual differences between the Preemptive and the traditional audit come into relief. Traditional auditing theory distinguishes between internal accounting controls—likely to have an impact upon the presentation of the financial statements in accordance with generally accepted accounting principles—and operational (sometimes called administrative) controls that tend to have less direct importance from a financial audit perspective but can have an important impact upon management's decisions. In general, a financial auditor tests controls upon which he or she has chosen to rely in terms of restricting his or her substantive tests of accounts; such controls are likely to be primarily of the internal-accounting control variety.

In a Preemptive Audit the distinction between the two types of controls need not be made. (In any case, the emergence of sophisticated computer-based systems has made it increasingly difficult to distinguish between internal accounting and operational controls.) And, the Preemptive Audit is done up front, before money has been spent, and is concerned with issues of planning and risk management. As a result of considerable experience with reviews of operational controls and Preemptive Audits, we have identified a catalog of "preferred practices." As discussed elsewhere in this book, such practices are simply those that have been found successful. At best, these preferred practices provide guidelines rather than mandates. The implementation of a particular preferred practice or a particular control is of far less importance than whether an objective is likely to be accomplished. To put it another way, the Preemptive Auditor deals with the likelihood of achieving the objectives of control on a proactive basis, rather than with the minutiae of specific practices. Therefore, all controls that can be tested should be tested using computer technology where practical.

In the Preemptive Audit, the nature of the control tests depends to some degree on the phase of the audit at which the tests are applied. Two major phases may be distinguished: the planning, which covers the development of the preliminary control plan, and the compliance, which covers the monitoring of performance in relation to that plan. In the first phase, opportunities for testing may be limited; work may involve judicious reading of documents and holding of interviews to ascertain that preferred practices have been considered and that the system will incorporate controls which, on an exception basis, will flag departures from plans and targets before economy and efficiency can be impaired. In the compliance phase, however, the auditor is in a position to test transactions and to analyze the impact of significant events on cost, timing, and quality. There are tests for the functioning of controls and the completeness and accuracy of reports, as well as special tests aimed at identifying certain unfavorable conditions.

This same concern with owner objectives distinguishes the Preemptive Auditing approach to control deficiencies. The financial auditor is interested in the deficiencies from the point of view of the additional account-substantiation testing that the deficiencies will necessitate. The Preemptive Auditor is interested primarily in determining whether practices can be improved to reduce losses or mitigate other negative effects.

In the Preemptive Audit, time is of the essence—the auditor conveys deficiencies verbally, recommends what should be done, and takes a guiding role in corrective action. In a financial audit, the management letter represents an endeavor to apprise management of deficiencies; and to spur corrective action. (There has been a trend to issue management letters on a more timely basis so as to remedy deficiencies, thereby obviating the need for extension of substantive tests.)

One feature common to both financial and Preemptive Auditing is the desirability of conveying the impact of deficiencies on profits, and also where possible on amounts at risk, in quantitative terms. The absence of this kind of quantification is a serious handicap to owners in setting meaningful priorities for corrective action and in determining the resources to be committed to redressing deficiencies.

In a financial audit, substantive tests and other specific audit procedures are performed to enable the auditor to express an opinion on the financial statements. In the Preemptive Audit, similar tests and procedures are performed for the purpose of determining whether the controls are in effect and are functioning as planned. Here the question is whether unfavorable conditions, against which management is endeavoring to guard, have occurred. If the tests reveal such conditions, the next step is to determine whether the breakdown occurred because of the way the system was operated, or whether systems redesign is necessary.

Summary of Comparisons with Financial Audit

The most important difference between the traditional and the Preemptive Audit lies in the focus of the Preemptive Audit on the achievement of management's objectives, involving operational as well as internal-accounting controls. Testing of the functioning of controls in Preemptive Auditing tends to be more pervasive in the compliance phase than in the planning phase, which focuses on the evaluation of planning documents. The Preemptive Audit is designed to uncover deficiencies, and to convey them to management as quickly as possible, together with directions for corrective action.

The Preemptive Audit and the Operational Audit

As its name implies, an operational audit bears primarily on the nonaccounting aspects of marketing, production, procurement, and other operating "cycles." Like its financial progenitor, the operational audit may begin with a survey designed to identify areas of control weakness, followed by an in-depth examination of documentation.

The distinction between a financial audit and an operational audit is made clear by the following example. A client of the author's firm had long been paying a wide range of prices for various grades of lubricants used in substantial quantities. The higher-priced lubricants, costing 40 to 50 percent more than the others, contained additives purported to possess special properties needed for certain applications. A traditional auditor would have concerned him- or herself with the processing and approval of invoices pursuant to terms negotiated, and with receipt of the materials, in other words with the completeness of the vouchers supporting disbursements. The operational reviewer went far beyond this, to test the validity of the assumptions on which the higher prices rested. Impressed by the profit effect of the price differentials, the reviewer asked maintenance personnel to draw up and furnish technical and performance specifications for lubricants used on particular jobs. The result is best described in the reviewer's own words: "As soon as these specifications were submitted to us, it became evident that the costly additives had no value for most of the uses to which the lubricants were put. The lower-priced lubricants would have performed equally well."

The auditor's concern with whether the lubricants were satisfactory for the uses to which they were put without having redundant properties acquired at extra cost illustrates the orientation of operational auditing toward the objectives of control. In respect to this emphasis, the operational audit may be seen as possessing kinship with the Preemptive Audit, in whose compliance phase the emphasis is particularly evident. On the other hand, an operational audit is mostly performed on a historical or retrospective basis, whereas the Preemptive Audit—especially in its planning phase—tends to be forward-looking and proactive; thus a Preemptive Audit of the maintenance function would be directed to ensuring that technical and performance specifications were being developed as an aid to efficient maintenance and to cost-effective shopping.

Operational audits have been espoused primarily by internal auditors.* Although the concept is more than a generation old, there is reason to believe that its influence on internal audit practice in the United States reached its peak a few years ago and has recently been on a plateau. If so, the explanation may lie in what some theoreticians take to be a fundamental weakness of this kind of audit. Ideally, the operational auditor should function in a manner supportive of those in charge of operations. The operational audit, however, is conducted after the fact. The auditor assesses the effect of decisions in which he or she had no role; where an assessment is less than positive, it is bound to reflect to some degree on the judgment of those who made the

*The term "management auditing" is sometimes used instead of "operational auditing." The drawback of this expression is its implication that management itself is the object of the audit, that is, is audited by internal auditors under its control.

decision. Under the circumstances, it is only to be expected that operations management will come to view the operational auditor's support as highly dubious at best.

Equally important is the fact that Preemptive Auditing, by its nature, embodies correction as well as discovery, whereas operational auditing leaves the remedies to subsequent management action. The implementation of the auditor's recommendations is not always as easy as it might appear from the foregoing example of an operational audit. This was brought out in a recent study of operational audits in the public utility field, which revealed that, notwithstanding much sound and fury attendant on report issuance, the audits gave rise to relatively little meaningful corrective action or lasting benefits.

The Preemptive Audit and the Program-Results Audit

The program-results audit was pioneered by government with a view toward seeing that programs achieved desired results in a cost-effective manner. Like the Preemptive Audit, the program-results audit utilizes review and testing techniques derived in part from nonauditing disciplines. Although some successes were achieved with this type of audit, there is reason to believe that there are very few instances in which it has been effectively carried out. The problem lies in the absence of criteria and ground rules for evaluation. Deprived of these basic requisites for auditability, auditors are forced to fall back on makeshift expedients, such as trying to create ex post facto program objectives (by looking over the shoulder of the auditee) or to develop surrogate measurement criteria. (There are indications that the United States General Accounting Office, which has long been at the leading edge of audit technology, is likely to reemphasize the more traditional operational auditing, for which "economy and efficiency" are the catch words, in lieu of program results.)

These limitations pose no problem for the Preemptive Audit which embodies business objectives and preferred practices. The Preemptive Audit can be applied to reasonably self-contained programs involving management of capital investments, construction, procurement, or even corporate governance. It is the difference in timing—the Preemptive Audit generally being done on an up-front basis—that offers prospects for success exceeding that of the program results audit.

The Preemptive Audit and the Strategic Audit

The strategic audit deals with prospective data which contain a degree, often a high degree, of uncertainty. Emphasis is placed on risks, because understanding them is crucial to successful strategic planning. The Preemptive Audit also is concerned with risk and its management, although usually in a tighter time frame than the strategic audit.

To some extent deficiencies detected during a Preemptive Audit may be factors in the reformulation of strategic plans. The Preemptive Audit of the budget is an example. The budgeting process represents the mode of specifying annual financial targets to achieve an overall financial plan; the budget allocates resources to achieve corporate objectives in the most efficient manner. If individual budgets are unachievable, the cause may lie in the unworkability of the overall plan, in the budget planners' misinterpretation of management's objectives, or in a major deviation from established operational policies. In any case, the strategic audit will have to consider the results of the budgeting review for appropriate reflection in the financial plan.

The Preemptive Audit and the Social Audit

The social audit has been defined as "the measurement and communication of the acts of an organization as they affect the organization's various publics." These "publics" include stockholders, employees, suppliers, customers, regulatory bodies, the community, and society in general. The social audit aims at improving allocation of resources and providing information for management decisions. It does not provide an easy solution to the difficult problems of expressing the impact of social acts or relationships in monetary or other quantitative terms.

Although the business community as a whole has been slow to accept the new audit application, the social audit has been incorporated into the regulatory standards of agencies concerned with economic planning and development, especially those abroad, such as the European Economic Community and the Organization for Economic Cooperation and Development.

The Preemptive Audit has an element of synergy with the social audit. A vital function of Preemptive Auditing is risk management, which assesses the cost of potential legislation as well as the potential cost of failing to comply with existing legislation (e.g., in the form of fines and lawsuits). The results of this kind of analysis can influence the nature and location of projects.

The Preemptive Auditor's Orientation

Some years ago a large public accounting firm reviewed the operations of an airplane manufacturer in a search of illegal payments. On the whole, the results were meager. Yet, sometime later, when auditors of the United States General Accounting Office carried out a similar review, they found substantial questionable payments. The disparity in findings had nothing to do with professional skills, size of audit team, or duration of the audit (which in fact was less for the GAO). The difference was one of audit perception or audit sensitivity. The first team of auditors had an attitude of "hear no evil, see no evil, speak no evil"; the personnel of the GAO admitted to the possibilities of evil.

The point of this example is that the Preemptive Auditor should always keep an open mind. Equally important, he or she should maintain a positive or constructive outlook. Not to do so may be to ignore the forest in favor of the trees. A Preemptive Audit may be conceived of as a treasure hunt with spoils in the form of opportunities for cost containment, revenue improvement, and general enhancement of operations. The following case history deals with an audit carried out in this spirit.

A company engaged in the manufacture of colored tanks and bowls shipped these articles in tandem, a practice that necessitated huge wood-reinforced boxes costing $2 each. The practice dated from the time when control of the coloring process was imperfect and random pairing of items supposedly of the same color would likely result in shading disparities. To reduce these disparities, the company had the items paired by color-sensitive employees working full time. Even then, however, there was a marked tendency toward disparity in shading within the supposedly matched items, particularly the black ones. About 20 years ago, scientific advances made it possible to achieve uniformity of color. The company disbanded the color selectors, but did nothing about the packaging. Finally, after several years, a perceptive auditor detected the superfluity of the tandem arrangement and recommended packaging the items separately in cardboard cartons costing 10 cents each.

Common-sense orientation, and a desire to improve operations are critical in a Preemptive Audit. The Preemptive Auditor's version of "Veni, vidi, vici" might be "I was vigilant, I visualized, I verbalized."

Summary

Although the Preemptive Audit draws upon many conventional audit techniques, it takes an essentially innovative approach based on (1) reviewing prospective and executory transactions rather than completed ones and (2) covering all controls without distinction between internal accounting and operational controls. The Preemptive Auditor should, above all, maintain a positive attitude toward the individuals whose actions are being reviewed. He or she should have a genuine desire to assist such individuals to more cost-effective and timely performance. And, the auditor should draw on the best talents of those individuals in finding timely and cost-effective problem solutions. Consequently, it is important for the Preemptive Auditor to convey findings without delay so that problem areas can be addressed.

CHAPTER THREE

General Techniques
of the Preemptive Audit

As mentioned, a Preemptive Audit has two phases, not necessarily discrete, (1) the planning phase and (2) the compliance phase. Certain general techniques apply equally to both phases.

Preferred Practices

Evaluations of control practices are carried out by utilizing benchmarks of "preferred practices." When a preferred practice that can adduce to the achievement of a particular objective has not been implemented or is being improperly implemented, and there is no evidence of other practices serving to compensate for the deficiency, the auditor makes a preliminary assessment of the dollar effect of that deficiency. If the deficiency is significant, he or she makes positive recommendations to solve the problem.

A word of caution is in order. As already mentioned, a Preemptive Auditor is not oriented toward application of specific practices, but toward achievement of broad objectives. Since it is impossible to specify techniques that may be appropriate in all instances, the preferred practices can only be seen as guidelines, not as inflexible mandates.

A second word of caution pertains to the evaluation of control needs. That evaluation must take into account the costs of installing and operating the controls. (These costs depend on the objectives of the controls—that is, prevention of errors, detection of variances, correction of deficiencies—and on the pattern of controls already established.) If, as sometimes happens, these costs outweigh the benefits anticipated from a control, the absence of the control should be considered tolerable. In recommending controls, the Preemptive Auditor's guiding consideration is, to use the vernacular, "getting the biggest bang for the buck."

The final word of caution relates to the evidentiary standards that should govern the Preemptive Auditor's determination of whether preferred practices are being implemented relative to a specified objective. The danger of taking the word of those supposedly responsible is illustrated by the experience of the author in connection with the audit of a government agency. When the head of that agency was asked what steps had been taken to comply with affirmative action requirements (which if ignored or applied without substance, could result in actions by the cognizant authorities that would entail costly delays in agency projects), he replied, "That's taken care of." When asked to support the statement, he produced a letter written to a black legislative leader offering the agency's support for affirmative action. Although this document indicated some recognition of the problem, it hardly represented institution of a meaningful preferred practice. In this case, the preferred practices would have been to establish realistic goals based on the community labor market; initiate an action program involving contacts with minority groups; systematize the investigation of minority enterprise status claims by bidders; and institute warning devices to alert the agency to shortfalls in hiring before they could become damaging.

Precisely what represents evidence of a preferred practice depends, in part, on the nature of the practice. Some practices are evidenced by documents, such as policies, procedures, letters, or operating instructions; others by physical manifestations, such as guards, fences, or locked doors; and still others by features built into a system, such as a programmed limit or a similar computerized instruction. Whatever form the evidence takes, it must be carefully examined. The example involving affirmative action illustrates the importance of perceptive evaluation of documents. In the same way, security arrangements should be observed directly and their function verified by questioning persons associated with them, and computerized controls should be tested by such means as a test deck or by running "tagged" transactions through the system.

Dollarization

When an auditor encounters a deficiency—that is, noncompliance with a preferred practice—associated with a particular objective, he or she must, whenever practical, determine how much money has been lost, or has been put "at risk." This technique can be termed "dollarization." Dollarization requires getting a complete understanding of a condition, determining whether the condition can be measured in monetary terms on the basis of available records, and assessing the value of the assistance that the persons whose activities are audited can be relied on to furnish (their judgment, in the absence of usable records, being often the best input the auditor has). The approach must be systematic, cost-efficient, and timely.

The importance of dollarization is difficult to overestimate; the technique may be applied to violations of preferred practices, significant events that may arise, and systems breakdowns. Assume, for example, that contractors on a construction project in progress have asserted claims based on the allegation that the owner did not properly coordinate the project. The auditor determines whether the claim has validity, and if it does, advises how the problem can be solved, if necessary by alternative approaches, and estimates the related costs and benefits. In addition, he or she may advise action (possibly systems revision) necessary to preclude additional coordination problems.

Commonly claimants want the owner to use additional labor to relieve their pressures; such labor typically involves overtime or a second or third shift. It may, however, be possible to bring the project back on schedule at comparatively modest cost by resequencing operations or by performing operations in parallel that previously were planned for sequential performance. Each approach has differing costs, benefits, and intangible attributes. The important point is that the auditor should be able—perhaps with the assistance of others—to make "quick and dirty" estimates of the results, not only of failure to install preferred practices but also of the corrective steps taken.

An important caveat in connection with dollarization is simply this: Apply common sense. It is axiomatic that corrective action will not be initiated until "dollarization" has brought the impact of a delinquency into focus. Under the circumstances, Preemptive Auditors may be tempted to simplify the procedures, engaging in unjustified guesswork, or abridging (or otherwise stinting) the computations needed by those who are charged with initiating corrective action. Contrariwise, Preemptive Auditors may "reach" for contrived, unrealistic, or excessively structured dollarization. Both extremes should be avoided. In general, auditees represent a prime resource for suggesting realistic and effective dollarization.

Computerization

Precipitate declines in the cost of computer hardware have brought within reach benefits long foreseen from computerized management information systems (MIS). Today it is often feasible to manage capital projects via "dedicated" computer installations. There has been no equivalent decline in the price of computer software (nor, for that matter, has the development of software kept pace with that of hardware), but program packages have emerged that purport, among other things, to monitor the cost, timing, and quality of capital projects.

The following computer applications come to mind in connection with Preemptive Auditing: (1) calculations, such as those needed to select an optimum depreciation method; (2) forecasting designed to compute potential results as well as the consistency of actual transactions with trends and budgets; (3) simulation using mathematical models to forecast results under alternate scenarios; and (4) creation of integrated data bases that accommodate cost and schedule control and resource allocation.

Required Computer Skills of the Preemptive Auditor

The Preemptive Auditor does not have to be a systems analyst or programmer. He or she should, however, be familiar with available hardware, and with relevant new developments in hardware technology, as well as with programs suitable for the Preemptive Audit, their technical characteristics, and their cost. (In the case of commercial program packages, selecting the one that best suits a particular set of circumstances is no easy task.)

In addition to this kind of formal knowledge the Preemptive Auditor must have a certain amount of EDP "savvy." Thus he or she should be able to synthesize hardware and software to achieve the optimal combination for audit needs. Another challenge the Preemptive Auditor must meet concerns software suppliers. Escalating costs and inadequate service (the latter often exemplified by failure to monitor program quality or the extent of the programming efforts) are the dangers of a too-casual approach to contractual relationships. The Preemptive Auditor should be very cautious about accepting open-ended contracts, and in drawing up a contract should make sure that deliverables and timing are spelled out and that there is ample provision for quality control and for definitive checkpoints and potential "holds."

Finally the Preemptive Auditor must be able to derive a sound working estimate of control needs, including internal accounting controls (which promote accuracy, timeliness, and completeness), and access and security controls. (It may be possible to have various departments check each other's work by having each department check its input, which may represent output of another department.) Access controls restrict human movements in order to reduce the chances of error or fraud; such controls, which should extend to all aspects of computer operations, are structured around a hierarchy of security classifications.

In setting up a computerized system or adapting an existing system to the needs of the Preemptive Audit, the reviewer should work closely with systems analysts and EDP technicians. In many cases, the reviewer will find it expedient to assemble an interdisciplinary team to expedite the process.

Mathematical Applications

Thanks largely to computerization, it is now possible to employ sophisticated mathematical techniques in financial analysis. Essentially, these techniques involve evaluating the implications of hypothetical alternatives, an approach sometimes referred to as "what-if" analysis. In the Preemptive Audit, this type of approach is commonly used for evaluating the cost and timing effects of corrective actions. For example, in a construction project, the corrective action might involve changing operational sequences or rescheduling major phases. With the aid of a computer, the results obtained under various operational patterns can be shown in mathematical models, from among which the optimal pattern may be chosen.

A particularly ambitious application of "what-if" analysis is decision theory which makes it possible to evaluate a decision on the basis of probable external events that would affect operations. A discussion of decision theory is outside the scope of this book. Suffice to say that in applying this sophisticated technique, Preemptive Auditors should be aware that their judgment will be colored by the way in which they perceive risk, and accordingly they should try to assess this bias so that it can be given proper weight in the analysis.

Also of value to the Preemptive Auditor, especially in the compliance phase, is regression analysis, which can be used to predict appropriate account balances and to determine and evaluate as a basis for action differences between actual balances and those predicted.

As in the case of computer technology, the Preemptive Auditor does not need a deep understanding of mathematics. (The more complex mathematical exercises can be designed and applied by trained professionals.) The auditor should, however, be sufficiently well versed in the implications of various approaches to ask informed questions and to suggest the use of a particular technique.

Communicating Audit Results

The findings of the audit should be conveyed initially to those immediately involved in the audited activities. Shortly afterwards, the audit results should be reported to the next level of supervision. At this level, the report should be accompanied by suggestions for corrective action, which, whenever possible, should cover several alternatives, with the advantages and drawbacks of each explicitly set forth. The time allowed for response to the reports will vary with the nature of the problem and·the scope of the measures proposed. In many cases, no more than one working day will be sufficient. It should be made clear to the respondents that they are being invited to consider only the proposed corrective actions, not the findings on which the recommendations are based. (If the audit has been properly carried out, unanimity on the findings should already have been achieved.) If possible, the corrective actions should be implemented without a formal report. If a formal report is deemed necessary, it will of course describe the planned or implemented corrective actions.

Relations with Auditees

A constructive attitude is a prerequisite to success in Preemptive Auditing. This attitude, in the form of a desire to help people improve their performance, should be apparent to everyone the auditor comes in contact with, whether in interviewing, conducting critical reviews of documentation or compliance tests, reporting findings, or formulating—in cooperation with the auditee—corrective actions.

Without the full cooperation of the auditee, the Preemptive Audit will be extremely difficult to carry out and the implementation of auditor's recommendations in an acceptable time frame virtually impossible. The key to this cooperation is trust, a trust that cannot be achieved unless the auditor cultivates a capacity to view matters from the perspective of the auditee. This idea was sagely expressed by an old Indian chief who referred to it as "walking in the other man's moccasins."

Summary

In this chapter we have presented a broad survey of generalized techniques of which a Preemptive Auditor should be aware: preferred practices, dollarization, computerization, participative management, and mathematical models. In subsequent chapters we will consider specialized techniques of particular interest to the Preemptive Auditor. It now should be apparent that Preemptive Auditing is not traditional financial auditing, nor is it management consulting, although it has elements of both. The chief thrust of Preemptive Auditing is toward early, pragmatic, and continuous corrective action. Preemptive Auditing is not investment management, project management, or construction management; this control-oriented new approach is directed toward seeing that doers follow good preferred practices, that they take timely and effective action on unfavorable conditions, and that such actions are subject to effective oversight.

CHAPTER FOUR

Specialized Techniques—The Preemptive Audit of the Planning Process

Before beginning the Preemptive Audit of the planning process, the reviewer should obtain an understanding of the organization's approach to planning. Is planning carried out in a participative manner, that is, do both top management and subordinates play their proper roles, or does management act without adequate staff work by subordinate managers or, conversely, relinquish too much responsibility to them (i.e., by accepting their work with too little study)? In consulting with subordinates, does the planning team rely equally on the views of staff people, engaged in such activities as research and development, human resources management, and financial administration, and of line people engaged in such activities as marketing and production? If not, which does it favor? What is the working relationship, if any, between the planning team and line managers? Is there proper communication between the two? Do planners make much use of up-to-date analytical methods, such as simulation and econometric forecasts, or do they rely on "gut-level" thinking? Are plans adequately reviewed? (If the operation is international, the above questions are applicable to overseas operations as well as domestic.)

What the Preemptive Auditor Looks For

Once the company's approach has been mastered, the Preemptive Audit of the planning process may begin. From the point of view of the Preemptive

Auditor, planning is, in general, the beginning stage of a managerial process that should include carrying out of plans, monitoring of performance in the light of expectations, accounting for results and variances, and evaluation of both performance and planning effectiveness. Proper planning involves:

1. Establishing general goals, dealing with corporate purpose and mission and organizational values.
2. Analyzing current and future environmental conditions.
3. Assessing corporate strengths and weaknesses.
4. Establishing specific objectives.
5. Developing the plans.
6. Securing agreement among the planners.
7. Disseminating plan provisions.

Of the above actions, the most problematic seem to be numbers 4, 5, and 7.

Establishing Objectives

Goals must be specified with precision. If the task of formulating them is assumed by top management, the participation of lower echelons that will have responsibilities in connection with the goals is vital. If, conversely, the goals are formulated by junior personnel, they must have adequate guidelines from above. Specific persons should be made responsible for overseeing efforts in connection with particular goals.

Developing the Plans

A plan is no better than the assumptions on which it is based. An assumption, in turn, is valid only to the extent that it takes into account external constraints. Suppose a municipality has decreed guidelines for parking facilities ancillary to certain types of public buildings—a convention center, for example—any assumptions concerning what is permissible in the design and construction of such buildings would have to take these guidelines into account. (Ultimately, compliance with these and other mandates of a city planning commission should be determined as a part of overall project evaluation.)

Both the plan itself and the assumptions on which it is based must be written, and in the case of the assumptions, documentation is necessary as well. No matter how brilliantly conceived and thought out a plan may be, it will suffer in the process of implementation if it is not explicit.

Disseminating Plan Provisions

The elements of the plan must be made known to all parties actively involved with them. Consider what would happen if engineers, assigned to design a series of bridges along a projected railway, were not informed by project planners that power was to come from a catenary (overhead) source. There would be a good chance that the bridge designers would fail to allow enough space to accommodate the overhead wires, a situation that could knock the original cost estimates for the line out of the box.

Risk Management

To plan for a capital investment and bring it to completion requires provision for risks, not only short term but long term as well. The principal risks that a business must contend with are external; examples are energy shortages, inflation, and competition. But internal risks, such as those involving the inability to make deliveries, cope with technological change, or meet quality standards, must also be taken into account.

To some extent, risks can be avoided entirely by careful planning. Those that cannot be avoided must be assumed (which is normally done unwillingly except where the potential loss is deemed insignificant) or shifted, either to other entities connected with the project or to an insurer. (Insurance covers only risks in excess of a deductible.) Even when management succeeds in shifting the risk, however, it still has an important stake in keeping down losses in any area of a project with which it is associated. Where there is insurance coverage, loss claims may result in higher rates. Where risks are assumed by contractors, there is always the possibility that a contractor will not be able to make good, in which case the owner will almost certainly be penalized. (Wrap-up insurance, under which one carrier handles a particular type of risk for the owner, regardless of whose immediate jurisdiction the loss is incurred under, gives the owner greater control in reducing that risk.)

What has come to be known as risk management is predicated on the theory that, to some extent at least, unfavorable possibilities can be anticipated and their effects mitigated. According to one analyst, the basic steps in risk management are as follows:*

---

*J. Fitzgerald, "EDP Risk Analysis for Contingency Planning," *The EDP Audit, Control and Security Newsletter,* September 1978, pp. 1–8.

List the potential causes of loss of the investment.

Estimate the value of the asset, or of related revenues to be protected, or the potential for cost increases or revenue losses.

Identify expected threats likely to cause loss.

For each threat estimate the probability of its occurrence.

Quantify the estimated loss.

Determine the approach to be taken to control.

Introduce the requisite safeguards.

In the case of external risks, the above approach requires the systematic gathering of intelligence external to the investor company, whereas internal risks are managed by analysis of the system itself with a view to incorporating appropriate flagging routines. As a project is implemented, it is necessary to perform a variety of tests to determine whether the external and internal controls are actually functioning and whether the unfavorable conditions to be guarded against are not indeed occurring. If they are, it may be necessary to modify the control system; in effect, a dynamic environment must be managed via nonstatic controls.

The following discussion deals with the principal risks that businesses face. For the most part they are external in nature.

Energy Shortages

The most typical approaches involve shifting the risk to the energy provider, via long-term supply contracts. It may also be possible to secure favorable rates from utilities by granting the right to interrupt service. Where interruption of service is not operationally feasible, it might be worthwhile for the company to build standby gas facilities which would enable it to take advantage of the reduced rates. This type of arrangement has been used successfully by a number of energy intensive industries, including a manufacturer of plumbing ware.

Material Shortages

The usual approach is to shift the risk to vendors via long-term contracts. Simply having more than one vendor to choose from may afford a certain degree of protection. Beyond this, it may be possible to share certain key materials with others in the same industry. Some companies in capital intensive industries provide an example of the successful use of this arrangement. As a matter of policy, these companies stand ready to supply other companies in the same business with temporary spare part replacements for crippled machines.

Inventory controls striking a calculated balance between acquisition costs, inventory carrying charges, and the need to protect the continuity of production may also reduce the impact of unplanned material shortages. There are computer-based mathematical applications that make it possible to determine the extent to which a company may be willing to assume the risk of stock-outs, while benefiting from reduced inventories. In the case of major machine spares, a reorder point system of zero might be appropriate. This calls for placing reorders only when the last spare is used; it also allows the company to hedge its bets via an emergency ordering procedure involving verbal purchase orders, subject to later confirmation, among other techniques.

Finally, a company in an industry given to material shortages can undertake a study to determine what if any substitute materials could be used, and what if any adjustments to maintain production and quality would be necessary with these materials. The results of the study could be embodied in a standby program, which in a crisis could be put into effect immediately.

Labor Interruptions

The possibility of labor interruptions is a realistic factor during both construction and subsequent operation. If union-shop contractors are to be utilized (i.e., in construction projects), it may be advisable to negotiate a no-strike pledge with craft unions. The owner should familiarize himself with the extent to which contractors are bound by strike notice clauses in national union agreements. (Such clauses may or may not be beneficial, depending on circumstances.) The presence of both union and nonunion labor on a project, especially a construction job, may create tensions requiring the exercise of diplomacy by management.

Once the job has begun, management must be constantly alert for conditions that might give rise to legitimate grievances, and must correct these conditions as soon as they are detected. To maintain this kind of awareness, the Preemptive Auditor can take the initiative in suggesting coordination meetings in which parties involved with labor management have an opportunity to air their views. Such meetings should be relatively structured in terms of agenda and minutes to make certain that all significant matters are noted and considered.

It has been the author's experience that labor has an interest in quality, especially where individual efforts are recognized (even if nonmonetarily) and is prepared to offer constructive suggestions. This contention is borne out by the success the Japanese have had with quality circles (worker-supervisor discussion groups), a technique that originated in the United States.

Inflation

It is often possible to shift the risk of inflation to vendors. One way to do this is to negotiate hard-money or fixed-price contracts; another is to limit or cap escalation in contracts. The author knows of one contract that specified that the balance-of-plant contractor was to be reimbursed for inflation at the regional Bureau of Labor craft index rates, or at 7 percent per annum, whichever was lower. During the life of this contract actual inflation ran between 12 and 15 percent. Capping of inflation risk may be possible even with the kind of raw materials that are subject to pricing as of the time of delivery (i.e., the so-called basic commodities) because discounts can be negotiated to involve ancillary services such as warehousing, special finishes, piecemeal deliveries, and other "customization."

A word of caution: The *owner* of a capital project must be alert to make sure that the risk of inflation is not shifted to *him* by an astute vendor. Apart from that, there is always the possibility that vendors will rebel against risk-shifting expedients.

Capital Shortages

It is necessary to synchronize cash inflow and cash outflow. Failure to achieve an appropriate approximate balance could invite either excessive cash balances or delays in payments to vendors. Particular attention of course should be given to cash outflows for material, labor, contractor financing, and mobilization. Relations with contractors, especially those involving cash payments, should be subject to tight surveillance and control. Thus when a bid stipulates that the owner assume excessive financing burdens on behalf of the bidder (a proviso commonly referred to as "front-end skew"), that stipulation should weigh against the bid. Also, owners should require vendors to submit preliminary estimates of cash drawdown requirements. Their subsequent requests for reimbursement should be monitored in the light of the planned schedules.

External borrowing requires careful analysis to fit company needs to available opportunities. Failure to borrow or borrowing from the wrong lender or under the wrong arrangements may constitute poor practice, especially where leverage is possible. (An owner's ability to control a capital investment through Preemptive Auditing may be used as a bargaining point in negotiating loans or credit lines; lenders may accept various periodic reports and representations, perhaps even with some mitigation of interest rates.) Managers of major capital investments are advised to familiarize themselves with available financing techniques, and to rank these techniques on the basis of tangible and intangible costs and benefits, to arrive at a choice. The importance of obtaining unbiased professional advice in connection with financing cannot be overestimated. That advice must be based on understanding of the owner's needs, accompanied by knowledge of the capital markets and of tax and accounting rules. A combination of investment (including bond marketing) and tax specialists may be needed.

Noncompliance with Laws

It is usually advisable to comply with a law rather than ignore it and run the risk of being brought into compliance at additional cost. Those in charge of capital investments are usually conversant with tax legislation of all kinds, but they tend to be less familiar with the regulations of government agencies, such as those dealing with money-market financing (e.g., the Securities and Exchange Commission), environmental protection (e.g., the Environmental Protection Agency), employee safety and health (e.g., the Occupational Safety and Health Agency), or employment of minorities. This ignorance can be costly in terms of time and money. In one case, the managers of a federally funded project, which required the award of a certain percentage of the total work to minority contractors, paid insufficient attention to the qualifications of the contractors selected to comply with this requirement. As a result, one such contractor—a large one—was decertified by a federal agency, thereby delaying the project by three months.

One way of coping with the regulatory maze is to have an attorney compile a list of laws, regulations, rulings, and court decisions that bear on the capital investment and use the compilation as a basis for monitoring against potential violations. Legal data bases now available for most states and for some foreign nations (particularly bases that provide the full text of legal documents) should be helpful to the attorneys in preparing this compilation. It is also possible to foster compliance by incorporating the compliance requirements in controls.

New Technological Requirements

Major capital projects are usually "state of the art," that is, planned on the premise that the latest technology will be reflected both in the design of the finished facility and in the techniques for constructing it. The pace of technological change being what it is, this factor accounts for a high proportion of cost overruns. Nuclear projects are a prime example of the havoc that the continuous demands of new technology can play with finite budgets—although here, a case can be made out for special budgetary latitude (a point of view that has yet to find favor with the public service commissions of several states).

Costs of technological change can be differentiated into costs of the new technology itself and costs resulting from functional obsolescence produced by the adoption of the new technology. When rendered unusable by functional obsolescence, materials, machinery, or structures must either be disposed of or modified. Disposition almost invariably involves loss, even when, as is frequently possible with materials, it is accomplished by sale or exchange. Modification, often possible with machinery and structures, of course entails expense.

Care must be taken to monitor technical change and to weigh its effects on costs over the investment's *entire* life. Assume, for example, that an investment involves the purchase of chipper blades to be used in a paper mill. If a new alloy of steel permits the manufacture of blades with greater resistance to wear, it may be cost-effective to shift to the new blades even if their purchase price is higher than that of conventional blades. Stated differently, it is possible that lower costs over the life cycle of the investment would more than compensate for the combination of installation costs and the extra cost of the new blades.

Competition

More often than is commonly realized the effects of competition can be anticipated and measured. Recently, a U.S. manufacturer of fabricated metals built an extensive facility in the United States for producing semifinished alloys. The raw materials used in the alloys came from a third-world country in whose manufacturing capabilities the American company had little confidence. As it turned out, management's skepticism was misplaced. Shortly after the U.S. plant became operational, a similar facility was opened in the supplier country and quickly established a clear competitive edge over the U.S. operation. Certainly, an in-depth survey to evaluate the productive capabilities of labor in the country where the metals were mined would have repaid its cost many times over. (The results of such surveys can be used to good effect in planning scenarios.)

New Legal Requirements

It is important that those responsible for overseeing capital investments or for bringing investments to fruition should consider potential as well as existing laws and regulations. The advantages of being able to anticipate with some degree of efficiency measures that can drastically affect any aspect of operations, would seem to be obvious. For example, if a law would have the effect of imposing certain mechanical, technical, or structural requirements, it is not hard to see why it would usually be much cheaper to accommodate these requirements *before* a project is completed than after. Yet surprisingly few companies have undertaken the necessary study to plan for legal and regulatory developments.

Consideration of these developments should not be confined to specific measures currently being deliberated by legislative or regulatory bodies. It should also embrace broad trends in social thinking that are *likely to produce* such measures, even if not in the immediate future. The kind of legislation that reflects such social thinking is illustrated by the so-called Vredeling Proposal currently being deliberated in the parliament of the European Economic Community. The proposal gives workers a share in decisions affecting their immediate welfare, and if enacted would be law in all the Common Market nations. (At present, legislative and other initiatives aimed at the welfare of workers, communities, and society as a whole are at a low ebb in the United States, but this condition appears to be in conflict with the broad evolutionary trend of our time.)

Thus, for the manager of a capital investment, the legal and regulatory environment should be defined in terms of *existing* laws or regulations that must be complied with and *potential* laws or regulations, including both those likely to become effective in the foreseeable future and those less likely to become effective but still worth consideration. In anticipating what is to come down the road and in matching the costs of modifying capital investments with potential benefits, probability mathematics—particularly as utilized in the prognostic approach known as decision theory—may be useful.

Summary

Risk analysis, as the term is used by a Preemptive Auditor, represents a broad endeavor to identify all possible causes of loss and to take appropriate management action relative to each. Very few potential losses are acts of God—careful planning can mitigate untoward effects in almost every instance. Obviously, the Preemptive Auditor must temper his or her concern for shifting risk to others with an appreciation for the interests of those to whom risk would be shifted; their financial health is also important to the owner, to say nothing of the need for attracting a broad selection of potential qualified suppliers of goods and services.

CHAPTER FIVE

Budgeting—The Importance of a Baseline Measure

In this chapter we will discuss the performance of a budget review. We singled this technique out for elaboration because of its innovative nature, and its importance to the Preemptive Audit.

Not many years ago, the author interviewed the chief financial officer of a large public utility engaged in constructing a nuclear project. When asked for the budget workpapers, this officer inquired: "How many hours have you got budgeted to review our budget?" When told we had budgeted 200, he responded, "I know where I can save you 200 hours." Indeed, in this instance nothing in the way of a budget had been put together; the chairman of the board had simply decreed construction of the facility, based on a "guesstimate" of $200 million. By the time the author's firm was called in to assess project status and the question of overruns, costs were approaching $1 billion.

Admittedly, this was an extreme example, although not as unusual as one might think. More representative was the situation at another company with which the author had direct experience. In computing its budgetary allowance for escalation of certain major construction contracts, management relied entirely on a general economic forecast. In so doing, it ignored the specific escalation provisions in recently negotiated contracts, provisions whose inflation implications were harsher than those of the forecast. Consequently, a significant upward revision of the budget became necessary.

Detecting and dramatizing the *absence* of a budget represents no challenge, but to be reasonably sure of uncovering weaknesses like those in the immediately preceding example, when working with detailed budgets that often give no outward indication of faulty preparation, the reviewer must do his homework and do it well.

Budgetary Assumptions

The importance of formulating valid assumptions has already been indicated in a general planning context. In budgeting, these assumptions are concerned essentially with costs, timing, and anticipated benefits. In budgets covering the entire investment period (as distinguished from those limited to a particular operating period), the assumptions most likely to be encountered are those dealing with:

Expected sales volume and price per unit.

Sales order backlog.

Inventory level.

Management policies.

Availability of labor and labor cost.

Availability of raw materials and raw material cost.

Productive capacity and the extent to which such capacity can be increased or decreased.

Kinds of financing available and interest rates.

General economic conditions.

Industry conditions, including competition.

Government policies, including tax matters.

It can be seen that these assumptions cover matters that are subject to many of the risks described in the previous chapter. For example, expected sales volume and price per unit are affected by competition. In evaluating these and other budgetary assumptions, the Preemptive Auditor should request from the budget team definitive statements pertaining to the expected events on which the assumptions are based. These statements are the products of risk analysis, which should be linked to the budget exercise. If management has been remiss in this respect, the reviewer may have to conduct risk analysis on a selective basis.

Main Points in a Budget Review

The Preemptive Audit of a capital investment must cover planning for compilation of the budget, budget organization, presentation, negotiation, and adoption of the budget, and above all the monitoring procedures and controls designed to facilitate budget execution. The following characteristics of a sound budget can serve as points for inquiry in a budget review:

1.   The budget should be accompanied by a written statement of assumptions and by data supporting estimates pertinent to materials, labor, and other factors. The assumptions should be documented, that is, sources should be cited (as by footnotes) whenever appropriate. Disclosure of assumptions greatly simplifies the task of isolating the reasons for any differences between results—in terms of cost, timing, and quality—and expectations, so that corrective actions, even if limited to future budgets, may be taken.

2.   There should be reasonable allowance for contingencies. A reasonable rule would be to base the contingency percentage on the degree of knowledge of the work to be performed, and on the related costs. For example, if a project involves a new rail line, and if there is a dearth of recent data on railroad construction, costs might be estimated by reference to roadbuilding. However, since relatively little is known about the parallel between railroad construction and roadbuilding, an above average—say 20 percent—contingency allowance would be appropriate. Further, if construction is involved, the budget should reflect the work breakdown structure. Because the time for project completion is an important factor in project cost, the cost–time relationship should be reflected clearly in the budget and continuously updated.

3.   The budgeting activity should occupy an important place in the hierarchical structure of the organization. The executive in charge of budgets should have clout, because he or she may have to act as an arbiter to resolve conflicting demands for scarce resources by competing organizational segments. For example, marketing people, who as a class are notorious optimists, may try to lay in a large inventory, whereas financial management may try to limit the aggregate inventory investment. In such a situation, the

budgeting executive may be called upon to establish compromise policies pertaining to stock-outs. As mentioned in the previous chapter, such policies may involve the planned assumption of stock-out risks resulting in lower inventory investments. The budget organization should prescribe the policies underlying budget fact gathering, compilation, review, and approval.

4. Budgetary control should be pervasive. In some organizations the capital budget is grafted upon an existing system without proper integration of budgets and accounts. With this arrangement, variances are not likely to be acted upon in a reasonable time frame, unless special precautions are introduced.

Another aspect of budgeting control deals with the relationship of the budget to responsibilities, and to responsibility accounting. In theory, people should not be charged with performance of activities over which they have no control. If, for example, the procurement department is expected to provide materials at a certain price, and the materials are to be installed by the maintenance department, purchase price variances should be charged or credited to procurement and not maintenance. Of course, waste or inefficient utilization of the materials would be the responsibility of maintenance.

To facilitate budgetary control a control model should be worked out and approved before work on the budget is final.

5. Budgetary targets should reflect stretch, that is, they should be set on the presumption that the highest levels of performance that can reasonably be expected will be achieved. (Here, the key word is *reasonable;* if a budget is overoptimistic, it may invite misapplication of scarce resources.)

This aspirational approach (commonly supported by incentives to employees) is really more defensive than aggressive. Without stretch, budgeting targets have a way of turning out to be too low, with inevitable depressing effects on performance.

6. The budget should be constructed in a manner that sets the stage for monitoring budget execution. For example, decisions must be made early as to which variances merit study from the point of view of project economy, timeliness, and quality. The list of appropriate variances will differ for different kinds of projects. For most projects, at least three or four of the following variances will be included: purchase price, quantity usage, labor price, labor efficiency, value earned, and overhead absorption.

7. It is important that periodic comparisons be made of actual cost to date plus cost of tasks yet undone, to the original budget as well as to the latest authorized updated budget. This involves a physical determination of

what has been accomplished, and what remains to be accomplished—a vital process that should help to alert budgetary planners, overseers, and front-line supervisors to possible budget overruns. (Readers should note that the operative word is *physical;* financial percentage of completion often will not provide sufficient basis for the determination.)

8.   Physical inspection is also necessary to keep track of the progress of critical structures, that is, structures necessary to the entire project (and generally identified as such in drawings). The inspections, which should be supplemented by other widely used scheduling tools, can be carried out by planners or by supervisory personnel.

9.   The budget package should reflect agreement among top management. True (as opposed to nominal) agreement on something as complex and ramified as a budget is only possible if there is a continuous two-way flow of information: directives downstream and suggestions and recommendations involving cost, timeliness, and quality upstream. It is not enough that budgetary planners approve an item and evidence their approval in writing; they must also, prior to approval, solicit the views of *all* those in a position to affect the success of the project.

10.   Where applicable precedents exist they should be consulted in preparing the budget. Assume, for example, that a public utility is in the process of modernizing its coal-burning plants through installation of new pollution-control equipment, and that the process has already been completed for two plants. By analyzing the original budgets and actual performance of the completed plants, planners undertaking modernization of a third plant should be able to frame their expectations more realistically than would otherwise be possible and thus arrive at a sounder budget.

11.   Significant revisions to the budget should be subject to the same pattern of control as the original budget. The more comprehensive the revision the higher the level of management that should be involved. Regardless of the extent of the involvement, however, controls should be in place to ensure that those charged with budget execution have been informed of each revision. They should also understand its nature and its importance in terms of how it affects time, cost, and quality performance measurements.

Phases of a Budget Review

Before beginning the budget review the Preemptive Auditor should enlist the cooperation of the person in charge of the budget. Next, the reviewer should try to obtain an understanding of the budget by studying budget policies, procedures, and operating instructions. He or she should then conduct interviews with both the budgetary planners and the front-line managers responsible for particular budget components. This understanding may be recorded by means of notes or flow charts. Although notes tend to be more cost-effective for short projects, the reviewer may employ flow charts if he or she wants to communicate that understanding to various operating departments, as might be desirable with projects of long duration.

The final phase of the Preemptive Budget Audit involves presenting findings and recommendations in accordance with the procedures described in Chapter 3 (under "Communicating Audit Results").

Summary

The "buzz words" for putting together an effective budget may be cited as participation of those concerned with budget execution, documentation especially of assumptions, reasonable contingencies, and a documented audit trail. Budgets should embody "stretch," that is, they should be attainable only with effort. And, contingencies should be based on knowledge of a particular area—if a great deal is known about an area, there would be a lessened need for contingencies; contrariwise, if an area is relatively unknown, substantial contingencies would seem appropriate.

PART TWO

Planning Phase

CHAPTER SIX

Planning and Budgeting

INTRODUCTION

The first stage in any project involves planning and budgeting. The basic concept of the project is embodied in an overall plan based on budgetary projections. The following activities characterize this stage:

Development of the project concept within an agreed-upon range of costs.

Preparation of a plan with provision for conceptual schedules; analyses of risk, financing alternatives, and constructibility; overall project organization and resource requirements; capital budgets and cash-flow projections; and other constituents of budgetary planning.

Establishment of program management systems including project cost control and management information.

Carrying out project engineering and value engineering, executing cost tradeoffs, prequalifying (i.e., prescreening) potential bidders, formulating terms for bidding (bid packages), and acquiring required permits and licenses.

OBJECTIVES AND TASKS

Evaluation of Investment Alternatives

Objective

Evaluate prefeasibility studies (that is, studies that evaluate the costs and benefits of alternative projects and alternatives to construction prior to carrying out a detailed site-selection study).

Tasks

Review the prefeasibility study together with supporting reports and studies to determine whether all substantive issues have been identified and evaluated and whether the findings of the study have the approval of all parties who should be consulted. The review should involve:

A. Inquiring of persons performing, reviewing, and approving the completion of research and the prefeasibility study to ascertain whether the procedures performed (and resulting reports, recommendations, and other documents) appear to be complete and appropriate.

B. Examining the prefeasibility study to determine whether:

1. Conclusions in the study are soundly arrived at and supported by facts.

2. Top management, the board of directors, or both, as appropriate, have reviewed and approved the study.

3. The following points were covered:

    (a) Technical feasibility (i.e., availability of materials, the required engineering and architectural expertise, access to raw materials and transportation, and proximity to markets and energy sources).

    (b) Availability of necessary construction and operations labor force.

    (c) Feasibility of the projected time for construction.

    (d) Licensing feasibility (i.e., in view of any environmental or political considerations or other factors that might affect licensing and thereby delay the project or prevent construction).

    Comment. The prefeasibility study may take anywhere from several weeks to several years to complete depending on the depth of the study and magnitude of the project.

C. Examining the documents comprehended by B for specific aspects indicated under each supporting study, as follows:

1. The cost/benefit evaluation, to determine whether the following were reasonable and proper under the circumstances:

    (a)   The method of evaluation used (i.e., cash payback, rate of return, net present value, discounted cash flow, or other).

    (b)   Nonrecurring start-up costs as well as continuing costs and benefits.

    (c)   Assumptions used (i.e., projected revenues and expenses, expected interest rate, adjustments for uncertainty, or other).

2.   The preliminary engineering estimate, to determine whether the following parties contributed to it:

    (a)   The in-house engineering staff.

    (b)   The architect/engineer, if appropriate.

    (c)   The construction planning consultant, if appropriate.

    (d)   The project manager.

3.   The financing study, for its effectiveness in evaluating alternative methods of financing the project, including:

    (a)   Bank loans (short or long-term).

    (b)   Credit lines.

    (c)   Private mortgage companies.

    (d)   Issuance of bonds, including feasibility and availability of tax-exempt bonds.

    (e)   Issuance of preferred or common stock, or both.

    (f)   Leasing.

    (g)   Federal or state funding (guarantees or direct loans).

    (h)   International lending agencies.

    (i)   Duration of financing.

    (j)   Contractor retention percentage.

    (k)   Contractor loans or joint financing.

4.   The preliminary study of risk management (the identification, quantification, and management of major risks) to determine whether the following parties were consulted in preparing the study:

    (a)   The project manager.

    (b)   The architect/engineer (if appropriate).

    (c)   The construction manager (if appropriate).

(d) The general contractor (if appropriate).

(e) The officers with jurisdiction over accounting, finance, or taxation.

(f) The legal counsel.

(g) The insurance manager.

D. Examining:

1. Management infrastructure to determine whether the owner has the capability and capacity to build the proposed facility.

2. The adequacy of existing operational and management controls in light of project needs.

Evaluation of the Costs/Benefits of Differing Sites

Objective

Evaluate the site selection process.

Tasks

Review site selection reports and recommendations to determine whether all substantive issues affecting the selection have been identified and evaluated and whether the site selected has the approval of all parties who should be consulted. The review should involve:

A. Inquiring of persons performing, reviewing, and approving the completion of research and evaluation to ascertain whether the procedures performed (and the resulting reports, recommendations, and other documents) appear to be complete and appropriate.

B. Examining the site selection research to determine whether:

1. Conclusions reached are soundly arrived at and supported by facts.

2. Top management or the board of directors, or both (as appropriate), have reviewed and approved the study.

3. Pros and cons of alternative sites have been considered in light of the following factors:

(a) Demographics.

(b) Legal and regulatory requirements.

    (c)   Proximity to, or availability of, sources of material.

    (d)   Proximity to markets.

    (e)   Environmental and licensing constraints.

    (f)   Competition.

    (g)   Costs:

Transportation

Material and energy

> *Comment 1.* Weather is a factor in both construction and operating costs, through its influence on energy costs and in other ways.

Labor

> *Comment 2.* Labor supply and its dependability, including union relations, affect both construction and operations. Problems will arise when there are labor shortages or labor unrest. They may also exist when there is an oversupply of labor, because even though wage rates may be lower, the saving may be more than offset by a drop in productivity resulting from the tendency of workers to cling to their jobs for as long as possible.

    (h)   Quality of life for employees.

Management of Risks

Objective

Determine whether all major risks have been properly provided for.

Comment 1. These risks include (but are not limited to) uncertainties connected with licensing, inflation, labor unrest or shortages, material shortages, delays in financing (especially in federal funding), legal challenges, environmental questions, financial and technical shortfalls of the contractor, energy shortages, weather, organizational coordination and communications problems, casualty losses, delays in design, scope changes, insufficient cost estimates or budgets, cost overruns, and employee fraud or other irregularities.

Item. A public utility negotiated a $150 million general construction contract for a generating station. The low bidder projected an annual inflation rate of 5 to 6 percent, based on a national economic forecast. The utility, on the basis of knowledge of its service area, believed that wage inflation—for skilled craftsmen—would run in excess of 12 percent. Accordingly, the utility opted for an agreement requiring it to reimburse the contractor for inflation at the rate shown by the Regional Bureau of Labor Statistics craft index, capped at a maximum of 7 percent per annum. Subsequent actual inflation ran in excess of 12 percent, involving an aggregate saving of over $10 million.

Tasks

Review procedures used to identify and manage major risks. The review should involve:

A. Inquiring of persons performing, reviewing, and approving the completion of risk evaluation to ascertain whether the procedures performed (and the resulting reports, recommendations, and other documents) appear to be complete and appropriate.

B. Examining final reports to management to:
    1. Determine whether the major risks have been identified together with steps for coping with them, and that the risk assessments have been approved by management.
    2. Evaluate the reasons given for the recommended risk management approach.

C. Examining reports and any supporting documentation:
    1. To ascertain whether the following have been consulted in identifying risks, as appropriate:
        (a) The construction manager.
        (b) The general contractor.
        (c) The project manager.
        (d) The architect/engineer.
        (e) Accounting, finance, and tax officers.
        (f) Legal counsel.
        (g) The insurance manager.

2. For evidence that, whenever possible, alternative methods of managing risks have been researched and the findings quantified.

3. For identification of all risk areas in which actual occurrences must be monitored.

D. Reviewing insurance policies and:

1. Comparing coverage to the results of the risk management study.

2. Assessing the effectiveness with which methods of reducing policy premiums have been utilized (for example through wrap-up insurance).

Comment 2. Under the wrap-up insurance concept, contractors and others who need insurance are protected by a single policy negotiated by the owner, instead of having to negotiate their own policies. The use of wrap-up insurance, where permitted by law, may save up to 50 percent of the total policy premiums and may result in better loss control. However, the concept has controversial aspects. Hence implementation should be preceded by comprehensive study.

Item. We suggested that a Midwestern railroad introduce wrap-up workmen's compensation insurance. Savings of approximately $2.5 million were expected, essentially by purchasing insurance at wholesale rather than retail prices. Further savings are likely to accrue because of the owner's improved control over losses.

E. Reviewing employee bonding arrangements for adequacy of coverage, with special attention to employees in the following departments:

1. Treasury.

2. Accounting; especially those employees involved in cash receipts and disbursements.

3. Purchasing.

4. Stores.

F. Examining policies and procedures for inclusion of:

1. Procedures for monitoring actual occurrences.

2. Follow-up procedures for mitigating the effect of adverse occurrences.
3. Procedures for periodically reassessing the risk management approach taken based on actual occurrences to date and projected occurrences in the future.
4. Provision for actual placement of insurance or establishment of reserves for self-insurance, as appropriate.

Evaluation of Financing Alternatives

Objective

Evaluate the adequacy of project financing giving consideration to cash-flow requirements.

Tasks

Review the financing arrangements and the cash-flow schedule, to determine whether they have been reviewed and approved by the appropriate parties; assess soundness and completeness. The review and assessment should involve:

A. Inquiring of persons performing, reviewing, and approving the completion of the financing evaluation to ascertain whether the procedures performed (and the resulting reports, documents, and recommendations) appear to be complete and appropriate.
B. Determining whether:
1. All financing arrangements have been reviewed and approved by top management or the board of directors, or both, as appropriate.
2. The cash-flow schedule and related research and evaluation have been reviewed and approved by appropriate supervisory or management personnel.
3. The construction manager or general contractor or both collaborated with management in developing cash-flow requirements (by examining documents used in developing the requirements).

Comment. Contractors prefer not to finance the construction work they perform, but instead to be paid for their work before they are required to pay *their* liabilities, an arrangement termed "front-end loading." So-called draw systems, wherein the contractor withdraws funds as needed, tend to invite front-end loading. With proper evaluation of cash takedown requirements by bidders on significant contracts, management should be able to minimize total construction and interest costs resulting from front-end loading.

C. Inquiring of the construction manager, the general contractor, or both, as to the nature and extent of his or their role in developing the cash-flow schedule.

D. As appropriate, examining documented research and evaluation supporting the cash-flow schedule and checking the results of the research and evaluation against the sources cited.

E. Trying to evaluate the reasonableness and propriety of the cash-flow schedule on the basis of approved construction scheduling requirements.

F. Evaluating financing agreements (for example, the mortgage or note payable and the lease agreement) before they are signed, for completeness and propriety and comparing their timing to the cash-flow schedule.

G. Checking current financing arrangements against the results of the financing study done as part of evaluating the cost/benefit of the proposed facility (for example, to determine whether tax aspects and federal and/or state subsidy opportunities have been considered).

Development of a Master Plan

Objective

Evaluate the project plan (mission statement).

Tasks

Review the project plan to determine whether it has been approved by all parties who should be consulted, defines the fundamental objectives to be achieved, and has been effectively communicated to all appropriate parties. The review should involve:

A.   Inquiring of persons performing, reviewing, and approving the completion of the plan to ascertain whether the procedures performed (and the resulting reports, recommendations, and other documents) appear to be complete and appropriate.

B.   Examining the project plan:
   1.   For evidence of approval by top management and, if appropriate, by the board of directors.
   2.   To determine whether the following are covered in the plan:
      (a)   A description of project.
      (b)   An estimate of project cost.
      (c)   A timetable for completion.
      (d)   The policy in regard to licensing.
      (e)   The approach to construction management (e.g., general contractor versus construction manager).
      (f)   The policy regarding status of drawings as condition for beginning construction.

> *Comment 1.* The policy may be to avoid starting construction in any area of a project until all the designs for that project are complete, or alternatively to permit construction in localized areas as soon as the drawings covering those areas have been completed, without regard to the status of the drawings for other portions of the project. The latter approach, termed "fast track," may be advantageous to the owner in that the project can be completed more quickly due to the overlap between the activities of the architect/engineer, and general contractor. Although control problems are increased under this approach, cost savings are possible if the architect utilizes suggestions from the general contractor and specialty subcontractors concerning more economical construction approaches. In addition, construction contracts can be signed at an earlier date conceivably lowering construction costs. The disadvantage of the fast-track approach is that only an experienced owner or construction manager will use it

effectively. Overlapping or duplicating work is a special hazard. Accordingly, stringent precautions must be taken to control drawings prepared and quantities physically moved or installed. Coordination among all parties is critical.

(g) Provision for review of all contracts by appropriate functional departments prior to signing.

(h) A definition of contractual and operating relationships between the owner and construction contractors, subcontractors, or the construction manager.

(i) A definition of responsibilities (internal and external) for management of all project functions accompanied by an organization chart showing all key positions.

Comment 2. Responsibilities for some functions could be assigned outside the organization; for example, the construction manager or general contractor could be assigned responsibilities for materials management. The owner, however, should always exercise active oversight and document his involvement.

(j) Provision for a procedures manual, listing in fine detail, responsibilities for each engineering, design, licensing, or construction item and how responsibilities between the owner, architect/engineer, construction manager, and contractors interface.

3. For logical arrangement, clarity, and usefulness as a communications tool.

C. Reviewing the intended or actual distribution of the project plan to determine whether all departments, plus any other parties concerned with any aspect of the plan, have been fully informed about their responsibilities.

Allocation of Adequate Resources to Budgeting

Objective

Determine whether sufficient resources have been allocated to the planning and budgeting function and that the function is properly structured and staffed.

Tasks

Review job descriptions to determine whether they have been approved by the parties that should be consulted and that they are appropriate in light of project objectives. The review should involve:

A. Determining whether job descriptions:
   1. Have been reviewed and approved by appropriate parties.
   2. Are accompanied by performance criteria.
   3. Adequately cover the duties and responsibilities associated with the planning and budgeting function.
   4. Tally in number and nature with the jobs on the organization chart.
B. Reviewing screening techniques for evaluation of applicants.
C. Determining whether recommendations for hire are supported by sound reasons (which must be documented) and that the recommendations have the approval of responsible officials.
D. Comparing actual hiring rates to scheduled hiring rates to evaluate the adequacy of job coverage.

Creation of a Procedural Framework for Budgeting

Objective

Evaluate planning and budgeting policies and procedures.

Tasks

Review policies and procedures relating to the planning and budgeting function to determine whether they address all significant aspects and have been approved by the appropriate parties. The review should involve:

A. Examining evidence that policies and procedures have been reviewed and approved by all levels of management concerned.
B. Examining policies and procedures to determine whether:
   1. Policy objectives are stated.
   2. Responsibility and authority are defined.
   3. Project and individual performance indicators are identified.

4. Procedures have been established for amending performance indicators including budgets to reflect changed circumstances.

5. Actual performance is continually monitored against performance indicators.

6. Performance is appraised.

7. A system of reporting requirements has been laid down to meet the needs of management and functional departments.

8. All laws and regulations have been complied with.

9. There is provision for:

    (a) Input and report formats.

    (b) Standard forms.

    (c) Internal controls (in terms of accuracy and completeness of reporting and in terms of encouraging efficiency).

    (d) Updating and approvals.

    (e) Quality control.

C. Scanning policies and procedures in general for logic and consistency.

Realistic and Documented Budgets

Objective

Evaluate the assumptions, estimates, and other input used to develop project budgets.

Comment 1. Project budgets generally fall into one of three categories: conceptual, preliminary, and definitive. Conceptual budgets are generated during the period of the feasibility study and are very rough estimates. The preliminary budget is drafted after preliminary or conceptual design activities have been completed but before detailed design has begun. The definitive budget is generally completed after at least 40 percent of the design work is complete. The conceptual budget is naturally the least accurate and the definitive budget the most accurate; the latter generally falls within ± 20 percent of performance.

Item. The chairman of the board of a Midwestern utility decreed, "There shall be a nuclear power station." However, the $200 million cost estimate was based exclusively on management's perception of what such a project might cost; no effort was made to develop documentary support for the estimate. Actual costs were fivefold the nonrigorous estimate. Lack of a meaningful estimate deprived the company of a gauge to detect out-of-line costs.

Tasks

Review the budget to determine whether it has been approved by the appropriate parties, is supported by research and evaluation, and appears to be reasonable under the circumstances.

> *Comment 2.* Amounts budgeted should reflect a certain degree of "stretch." The amounts should not be so difficult of attainment, however, as to discourage superior performance. To the extent they are, they should be amended. There also should be sufficient documented "links" between the original budget and all budget amendments. Finally, budget estimates should be detailed enough to mirror actual construction activities.

The review should involve:

A. Inquiring of persons performing, reviewing, and approving the completion of the budget to ascertain whether the procedures performed (and the resulting reports, documents, and recommendations) appear to be complete and appropriate.

B. Determining whether the budget has been reviewed and approved by top management for general content and by appropriate supervisory personnel for accuracy.

C. Examining supporting documents to see whether all reasons supporting conclusions are documented and that alternative methods, concepts, and approaches have been considered and evaluated.

D. Trying to assess:
    1. The propriety of conclusions based on documented evaluations and approved budget estimates.
    2. The completeness, reasonableness, and propriety of budget assumptions:
        (a) Economic: The estimated inflation rate and interest rates.
        (b) Functional: Constraints imposed by existing facilities and equipment on proposed construction.

Comment 3. For example, consider an oil company contemplating construction of a new refinery with three times the capacity of its existing refineries. It must weigh whether it has tankers with enough capacity to allow the refinery to operate at the planned percentage of capacity, possibly 100 percent.

Item. Individuals starting to prepare a budget for new rail trackage had not recorded their assumptions; designers of bridges were contemplating a diesel-powered line; those planning vehicle acquisitions envisioned an overhead catenary system; these power systems have different design and cost impacts. Accordingly, all assumptions had to be synchronized, before work proceeded on the budget.

E. Determining whether budget estimates:
1. Have been reviewed and approved by appropriate management personnel.
2. Are supported by research and evaluation.

F. Assessing the accuracy and validity of the budget estimates by reference to sources, including:
1. Material quantity estimates (based on drawing takeoffs; consultation with the general contractor, project manager, architect/ engineer, and other contractors with whom management has relationships; and experience with published standards as well as with the factors of pilferage and spoilage).
2. Material costs (based on such factors as supplier quotations; reference to catalog prices; escalated historical costs—that is, costs adjusted for inflation; bids; and contracts).

Item. For a Southern utility, we reviewed the definitive cost estimate for a generating station. The client had computed escalation on the basis of national economic forecast information. This methodology was followed, although purchase orders contained specific clauses for escalation for major items. The invalid approach resulted in underestimated escalation of $50 million. The Public Service Commission was notified of the error; on the longer-term basis the utility's credibility was enhanced. Furthermore, the correct estimate provided a valid gauge to assessment of subsequent performance.

3. Labor productivity estimates for use in determining labor hours (based on published estimates for the construction industry and on published engineering standards, as well as on recommendations of the construction manager, general contractor, project manager, architect/engineer, and other consultants).

4. Labor rate estimates (based on union labor rate schedules).

5. Overhead allocation estimates (based on the owner's escalated (i.e., inflation-adjusted) historical overhead costs).

6. Estimates to cover administrative functions (based on projected manpower, supply, and overhead costs) including:

    (a) Planning and budgeting.

    (b) Contract administration.

    (c) Affirmative action.

    (d) Claims.

    (e) Internal audit.

    (f) Management information.

    (g) Accounting/finance.

7. Taxes, such as sales, use, and real estate.

    Comment 4. It is usually difficult to budget real estate taxes (if any) during construction. If necessary, consideration should be given to taxes not budgeted for when developing project contingencies.

G. Determining whether construction estimates prepared by contractors (i.e., material quantities) are evaluated for reasonableness by persons *independent* of the contractor and of others whose compensation is based on achievement of those estimates.

    Comment 5. Direct observation of procedures and questioning of personnel are the usual means of obtaining the information needed. (This step may not be appropriate, however, for an owner under a lump-sum contract.)

H. Evaluating the qualifications and competence of outside experts used to develop budget estimates (such as a professional engineer, architect, construction manager, or general contractor).

I.   Determining whether:

   1.   There are any circumstances that bear significantly on the reasonableness of budget estimates (i.e., pending union contract renegotiation or declaration of bankruptcy by a supplier's competition which could result in the supplier raising his own price) and trying to assess the effect of these circumstances on the budget.

   2.   Budget amendments are subjected to appropriate management review and that all reasons for the amendments are properly documented.

J.   As appropriate, assessing the accuracy and validity of new budget estimates by reference to sources and assessing the reliability of the sources, including their up-to-dateness.

   Comment 6.   All information used in budget estimates should be continually updated to the most current information available.

K.   Trying to evaluate the reasonableness and propriety of the escalation estimate and its application to all appropriate budget components (i.e., by reference to such sources as the commodity price index, published figures on industry escalation for the past several years adjusted for future projections, specific purchase orders and/or contracts where applicable, and others).

   Comment 7.   Average rates used over a number of periods may hide highs and lows, which, when undetected, can be disastrous if they occur at inopportune times.

L.   Assessing the reasonableness and current applicability of the financing studies (updated as appropriate), the approved construction schedule, and correspondence with financing institutions.

M.   Examining documents supporting the contingency estimate to determine whether all risks are addressed in the budget (by reference to prior studies) and to evaluate the reasonableness and propriety of the contingency estimate.

   Comment 8.   The major components of the project contingency estimate include design contingencies, construction contingencies (including casualty contingencies), and general economic contingencies. The amount of effort required to develop the project contingency estimate generally depends on the completeness of information obtained to develop the budget estimates and on the assumptions used to develop the budget. (Thus, the construction contingency factor should be less when the budget is prepared on completion of the design than when the fast-track method is used and the budget is prepared with only preliminary drawings completed for many segments of the project.)

Item. A railroad built the first new trackage in the United States in many years. Since little was known about railroad building in the current environment, parallels were sought to roadbuilding. We increased the contingency reserve on the premise that the less known, the greater the need for a cushion. The overall upward adjustment in the railroad construction budget involved close to 10 percent, or $50 million. The realistic estimate enhanced the road's posture vis-à-vis potential lenders, and its negotiating posture with the lender group.

Systematic Approach to Permits and Licenses

Objective

Evaluate compliance with licensing and regulatory requirements.

Tasks

Review licensing and regulatory policies and procedures and evaluate the measures taken to identify the requirements on which the policies and procedures are based. The review and evaluation should involve:

A. Determining whether legal counsel (either inside or outside) was consulted in identifying applicable federal, state, and local legal and regulatory requirements and examining all documents (including all correspondence) pertinent to these requirements and compliance with them.

B. Checking the policies and procedures against the above documentation.

C. Determining whether:

1. The policies and procedures take fully into account priorities and allowances for lead times in complying with the requirements (for example, by a compliance schedule).

2. The requirements of all regulatory agencies that might have jurisdiction over the project have been canvassed to make sure that no applicable requirements have been overlooked.

3. To the degree possible, the requirements of different agencies should be combined so that the needs of many agencies can be accommodated by relatively few passes through the records.

Comment. It may be necessary to negotiate with regulators to promote the acceptability of relatively standardized data to meet the needs of most, if not all. The investment in such negotiation/coordination will be repaid manyfold through a reduction in the repetitive clerical burden.

Effective Construction Oversight

Objective

Evaluate the project organizational structure.

Tasks

Review the project's organizational structure to determine whether it has been approved by the appropriate parties, provides for essential management functions, and maintains a proper balance between differentiation or specialization, on the one hand, and integration, on the other.

Comment 1. If management has experience with construction projects of comparable magnitude to the one under consideration, the results of that experience should not be lost sight of in performing this review.

The review should involve:

A. Determining whether the project's organizational structure has been reviewed and approved by top management.

B. Reviewing the method by which the organizational structure can be enhanced or enlarged.

C. Determining whether such functions of internal or external personnel as project oversight/management, construction management, contract administration, licensing, quality control, accounting, expediting, procurement, and design engineering, are provided for.

D. Determining which of the three recognized types of organizational structure, the functional, the project, or the matrix, applies to the project, and considering whether that structure is the most appropriate from the standpoint of cost effectiveness and personnel development.

Comment 2. In a functional organization, employees report to the head of a functional division such as engineering, manufacturing, marketing, or legal. The project manager has authority over the division heads but little or none over individual employees. In a project (vertical) organization, individual employees are taken out of the functional divisions and assigned to work full-time for a project manager. The third type of organization, the matrix, combines aspects of both of the foregoing; individual employees take technical direction from the functional divisions and project direction from the project manager. Personnel folders are usually retained in the divisions, but the project manager contributes to personnel evaluations. On large, complex projects, matrix organizations are generally most effective.

Item. A public utility's construction maintenance division undertook several hundred projects with an average value of less than $1 million; but, a $50 million modernization project was included in the total. Given the size of the project, and its importance to the continuity of operations, we suggested a separate matrix management approach for the large project. In this way those assigned to modernization were given *specific* responsibilities for success, in addition to their discipline-related tasks.

E. Assessing the extent to which the reporting relationships (determined by the organizational structure) facilitate timely and effective resource allocation.

Item. In investigating overruns incurred in construction of an auto assembly plant, we found that construction oversight had become a matter of jurisdictional strife between corporate engineering and divisional maintenance; consequently, day-by-day problems remained unaddressed. We showed the client how to solve the jurisdictional problem, and developed a control plan to be used on future projects.

Assignment of Comprehensive Design and Engineering Responsibilities

Objective

Determine whether design and engineering responsibilities have been properly defined and evaluate whether they have been appropriately assigned.

Tasks

Review design and engineering responsibilities to determine whether they have been defined, assigned, reviewed, and approved by the appropriate parties and whether they provide a sound basis for selecting the architect and the engineer (who may be one person) drafting the architect/engineer's (AE) contract, and establishing performance criteria for subsequent measurement of design and engineering effectiveness.

> *Comment 1.* In this section, it is assumed that all design and engineering responsibilities are assigned to an architect/engineer. However, on some projects, the owner may retain certain design or engineering functions or reserve the right to review and approve the work of the architect/engineer.

> *Item.* We reviewed controls over a waste-water treatment facility being constructed for a Southern city. The city had no engineers with the training necessary to monitor performance of its "turnkey" contractor. We recommended that the city hire a professional engineer to supervise the establishment of a realistic budget, and to monitor compliance with cost, quality, and delivery targets.

The review should normally involve:

A. Interviewing the persons involved in design and engineering and reviewing the policies, procedures, and operating instructions governing their functions to determine whether appropriate standards and rules have been established.

B. Examining contracts:
  1. With the design engineer, to determine whether contract content has been reviewed and approved by top management.
  2. With the architect/engineer, to determine whether the following design and engineering responsibilities have been appropriately covered.

Comment 2.   For ease of reference we have grouped these tasks under the headings of systems and procedures, planning and design, and construction. The initial entry under systems and procedures may or may not be assigned to the architect/ engineer, depending on the construction management arrangement.

(a)   Systems and procedures:

Creating an accounting control system.

Preparing current status reports.

Preparing reports, directives, and other data.

Establishing procedures.

Establishing a master schedule.

(b)   Planning and design:

Developing the engineer's cost estimate.

Preparing budget recommendations, specifically those in-volving lead times for procurement, quantity estimates, possible construction problems, and contingencies.

Preparing periodic cost projections coordinated with proj-ect progress.

Reviewing alternate design parameters and performing analyses to arrive at a recommended design.

> *Comment 3.*   In many cases such analyses require con-sideration of cost/benefit factors; therefore management should consider reviewing design recommendations.

Assistance in determining licensing requirements and in responding to such requirements.

(c)   Construction:

Reviewing or supervising construction activities to ensure that the intent of the engineering design is being fulfilled.

Consulting with the construction manager, contractors, or both, on interpretation of design documents.

Reviewing shop drawings.

Providing technical assistance in bid evaluations, as desired.

Providing assistance in connection with drawing or specification interpretations.

(d) Procurement:

Purchasing materials or equipment as specified.

Compiling and distributing the bill of materials.

Determining schedule requirements and necessary lead times.

(e) Design review process:

Formulating procedures for review of design calculations, design criteria, drawings, and specifications.

Comment 4. It is often beneficial for an outside, independent consultant to review the design process, to provide additional professional resources, and the benefit of an independent perspective.

Assignment of Comprehensive Construction Management Responsibilities

Objective

Determine whether construction management responsibilities have been defined and assigned with maximum efficiency.

Tasks

Review construction management (CM) responsibilities to determine whether they have been identified, assigned, reviewed, and approved by the appropriate parties, whether they define all significant CM responsibilities and whether that performance is reported and measured.

Item. For a West Coast hospital project we examined the terms of the draft contract with the construction manager; any savings below a CM-guaranteed maximum price were to accrue to the hospital. The arrangement did not provide a financial incentive to the construction manager to strive for savings. Shared savings would have the effect of encouraging the construction manager to work toward implementation of savings techniques and to be vigilant to inflated bids.

The review should involve:

A. Inquiring of the individual charged with supervising construction on the owner's behalf whether precautions have been taken to ensure appropriate assignment of responsibilities, and the related reporting of performance.

B. Ascertaining whether the definition and assignment of activities have been reviewed and approved by top management.

C. Examining the construction management contract for coverage of certain key responsibilities, as follows:

    1. In the area of systems and procedures, for:

        (a) Maintaining an accounting control system reflecting budgeted cost of function, contract, or significant building components based on a definitive estimate, together with actual cost and latest cost to complete, as well as explanations of variances and recommended managerial actions.

        (b) Providing:

            Current status reports covering projected activities, performance against prior period projections, cash-flow projections, and contract commitments.

            Reports, directives, and other data intended to assist the owner and other parties concerned in project administration and in compliance with federal, state, and local laws.

        (c) Formulating procedures (preferably embodied in a written manual), covering operating instructions, forms, and input documents, together with output reports and schedules.

        (d) Developing a master schedule (with appropriate allowance for lead times) that establishes major project milestones for planning, design, construction, and conceivably for preoperational testing and for moving employees and equipment into the completed facility.

        (e) Maintaining records covering contracts, shop drawings, subcontracts, machine operating instructions, maintenance handbooks, and other essential data.

2. In the area of planning and design, for:
    (a) Providing a means of identifying and managing risks (such as the possibility of labor unrest or material shortages).
    (b) Developing a project cost model.
    (c) Providing:

    Budget recommendations, specifically those involving lead times for procurement, quantity estimates, productivity factors, and contingencies.

    Periodic cost projections coordinated with project progress.
    (d) Assisting the owner in determining licensing requirements and in fulfilling them.
    (e) Reviewing the conceptual design and related documents, giving weight to the effect of materials on constructibility, on construction techniques and on cost, quality, and delivery.
    (f) Assisting the owner in interpreting design modifications and drawing refinements (in consultation with the architect/engineer).
    (g) Establishing procedures for creating, expediting, issuing, and controlling shop drawings.
3. In the area of contract administration, for:
    (a) Assisting the owner in:

    Developing contractual policies.

    Formulating the "pro forma contract" or "bidder's package" (with recommendations where appropriate).

    Handling broad bid solicitations.
    (b) Establishing prequalification criteria for bidders and suppliers.
    (c) Reviewing bidder qualifications, including inspections of shops.
    (d) Attending the prebid conference.
    (e) Reviewing bids and proposals, with recommendations pertaining to awards.
    (f) Selecting consultants and specialty contractors.

(g)   Managing materials including:

Expediting.

Receiving.

Storage and materials handling.

Value analysis.

(h)   Traffic management at the construction site and externally.

4.   In the area of construction, for:

(a)   Coordinating, supervising, administering, and directing contractors.

(b)   Reviewing, processing, and approving requested progress payment applications to ensure they are based on work actually accomplished and on conformity to contracts.

(c)   Conducting meetings to coordinate activities with contractors.

(d)   Measuring labor productivity.

(e)   Initiating recommendations for project changes giving appropriate consideration to the impact on cost, scheduling, and quality.

(f)   Preparing cost analyses and technical reviews (embodying recommendations, where appropriate) covering contractor-recommended changes, including drawings and specifications, accompanied by recommendations.

(g)   Providing assistance in connection with:

Interpreting contracts and drawings.

Dealing with claims asserted or actions brought by contractors relative to design or construction (with recommendations where appropriate).

(h)   Conducting tests and systematic observations to ensure appropriate quality of construction.

(i)   Inspecting contractors' work for conformity to appropriate construction quality standards, and rejection when called for.

(j)   Reviewing unsettled claims together with recommendations.

(k)   Carrying out cost audits.

5. In other areas, for:
    (a) Providing project office facilities; power; cleaning, maintenance, and pest control; and security.
    (b) Supervising, administering, and coordinating equipment installation.
    (c) Obtaining building permits and special permits.
    (d) Preparing occupancy schedules.
    (e) Coordinating contractor-shared facilities.
    (f) Providing preoperation check of utilities, operating systems, and similar equipment.
    (g) Monitoring relations with regulatory agencies, unions, contractors, and the community.
    (h) Administering equal opportunity and affirmative action programs.
    (i) Installing and operating safety programs.
    (j) Selecting and training of maintenance personnel.
    (k) Providing final inspection of the work together with appropriate recommendations and rejection where called for.

    Note. The above list of construction management tasks is not all-inclusive.

D. Reviewing construction management reporting requirements for inclusion of:
    1. Material on:
        (a) The nature and content of reports to be submitted.
        (b) The nature of evidence to be submitted in support of reports.
    2. A timetable for reporting.

E. Reviewing the assignment of construction management responsibilities to assess whether (1) the responsibilities have been properly defined, and (2) the assignees have the requisite capability and authority to discharge the responsibilities and are prepared to render full account of their activities in reports they can substantiate.

Comment. The important consideration here is that no construction management responsibility "falls between the cracks," as it were.

Striving for comprehensive coverage may be regarded as more important than who should perform a particular task. On the other hand, once an assignment has been made, the organizational unit or person responsible should have the authority and resources for effective performance. And, precautions should be taken to avoid overlapping and duplication.

Item. A major oil company constructed a regional office building. Responsibilities for monitoring design and construction were assigned (in triplicate) to the company's own project manager, the outside construction manager, and the architect/engineer. To avoid replication of the monitoring effort, and to limit disputes among the parties, we suggested concentration of the responsibility in one qualified provider of the service.

Performance Measurement

Objective

Assess the criteria for evaluating performance, not only of the project as a whole but also of individuals.

Tasks

Review project and individual performance indicators to determine whether they have been approved by the appropriate parties and encourage superior performance.

Comment 1. The factors of cost, timeliness, and quality by which performance is judged conflict to some degree. The most favorable level that can be achieved for each factor represents an optimum, somewhat below the level theoretically obtainable if that factor were independent of the other two. Such optimization represents an exercise in balancing. In assessing performance measurement criteria, it is important to be on the lookout for employment of such "speed-up" techniques as fast track or simultaneous design/construct, which are often implemented at the expense of control.

The review should involve:

A. Determining whether the performance indicators have been approved by top management.

Comment 2. Strictly speaking, an indicator is a variable relationship that measures performance at any level, for example miles per hour. However, as used in this book, "performance indicator" refers to a specific level of performance, not to the system or scale by which that level is determined; thus the term is virtually synonymous with goal. A basis of performance measurement should be established at an early stage for ready comparison with expected results as the project progresses. Most performance indicators apply to the construction phase of a project, but performance indicators should also be utilized in the areas of design, engineering, and licensing, wherever applicable. Performance indicators should be framed in such a way that meeting them requires a degree of "stretch," that is, extra effort. Standards should not be so unrealistically high, however, as to discourage superior performance. (Low standards also have a negative effect on performance.)

B. Examining the proposed performance indicators to determine whether they include the following:

1. For project performance, in terms of:

   (a) Cost:

   Original budget versus amended budget.

   Amended budget versus purchase orders.

   Actual cost to date versus budgeted cost to date.

   Actual man-hours utilized versus budgeted man-hours.

   Total estimated cost versus budget (i.e., actual costs to date plus estimated costs to complete versus budget), assuming an appropriate method for calculating estimated costs to complete.

   Costs incurred as a percentage of total budgeted cost versus physical completion.

   Actual cost savings utilized versus identifiable cost-saving opportunities.

   The cost of scope changes (by the architect or the engineer).

   The cost of further defining engineering or construction requirements.

   The cost of contingencies relative to estimates.

   The cost of settled claims relative to the cost of asserted claims.

Comment 3. Although the performance indicators outlined herein are project-oriented, they can (and should) also be utilized with large individual contracts, such as those with the architect/engineer, and construction manager, whenever applicable.

(b) Timeliness:

Actual progress versus expected progress for the entire project, and for significant project components (such as units installed to date).

Time-saving opportunities actually utilized as a proportion of total time-saving opportunities identified.

(c) Quality:

The number of quality exceptions in relation to the acceptable norm.

The number of inspections in relation to target.

The number of exceptions as a proportion of the number of inspections.

The number of clearances as a proportion of the number of exceptions together with timeliness of clearance.

Comment 4. In setting quality standards, a review should be made of previous construction failure experience (for example, past failures with steel and concrete contractors), so that these failures may be taken into account.

2. For individual performance (e.g., of contractors, functional departments, and specified personnel), in terms of:

(a) Cost:

Amounts disbursed for acquisition of materials, and for salaries and miscellaneous items (but excluding disbursements that could not have been reasonably foreseen) versus budgeted amounts for each.

Cost-saving opportunities utilized as a proportion of total cost-saving opportunities identified.

Cost savings originated.

(b) Timeliness:

Actual task completion time in relation to budgeted completion time.

Minimization of "negative float" (insufficiency of resources available to complete a specific project) in the critical path management (CPM) schedule.

Overtime.

Cost of contractor claims related to delays.

(c)   Quality:

The number of inspections, exceptions, and timely clearances in relation to the expected number.

Rework levels in relation to specified criteria, and reasons for the excess, if any.

Levels of rejection in various materials compared to expected levels.

The number of legal or punitive actions (i.e., court proceedings, dockings, etc.) resulting from poor work.

C.   Assessing the system for amending performance indicators to determine whether it provides for:

1.   Appropriate levels of management approval.

2.   Requirements for justifying the amendment of an indicator (i.e., facts fully documented with supporting data).

3.   Adequate documentation for any changes from a performance indicator.

D.   Making a tentative assessment of all performance indicators for inbuilt "stretch" and optimum combination of cost, timeliness, and quality within the framework of practicality.

Emphasis on Scheduling

Objective

Evaluate scheduling concepts, techniques, and approaches.

Comment 1. All major projects should have five types of schedules. The basic schedule covering key project activities is known as the milestone schedule. This schedule is usually provided by the owner. From this document, four other schedules are generated, covering engineering, licensing, procurement, and construction. Many jobs also require subtier schedules, covering such factors as cash flow, manpower, loading, and start-up. These schedules may be generated by several parties but they must be integrated into an overall project schedule.

Item. A large Eastern city selected a construction manager who lacked the professional capability, and the computer access, to schedule a large convention center. Consequently, an outside consultant had to be engaged on a "joint venture" basis. Cost and time controls were not fully integrated, creating coordination problems, and posing a hazard of contractor claims for owner-caused delays.

Tasks

Review the milestone schedule and any related subschedules to determine whether they have been reviewed and approved by the appropriate parties and that they seem reasonable.

Comment 2. Consideration should be given to the site's physical requirements, as well as to local economic conditions and the labor market. The construction manager and architect/engineer should establish the sequence of events based on an analysis of cost, quality, and delivery tradeoffs.

The thrust of management's review of the construction schedule should be to assess how completely and accurately the schedule reflects the underlying research. However, if management has sufficient engineering expertise at its disposal, it may also evaluate the *reasonableness* of the schedule.

The Preemptive Audit review should involve:

A. Inquiring of persons performing, reviewing, and approving the preparation of schedules to ascertain whether the procedures performed (and the resulting reports, documents, and recommendations) appear to be complete and appropriate.

B. Seeing whether:
1. The milestone schedule has been reviewed and approved by management (as attested by signatures of approval, documentation of the nature and extent of review procedures performed, memoranda relative to questions, and other evidence).

2. The alternative concepts, techniques, and approaches were investigated and pros and cons were documented, as follows:

(a) As appropriate, by examining documents supporting the concepts, techniques, and approaches, evaluating their accuracy and validity by reference to sources, and assessing the reliability of the sources.

(b) By examining all information relative to scheduling, for possible conflicts.

C. Determining whether:

1. "Explosions" of dates (detailed schedules prepared from basic target dates) have been reviewed and approved (as attested by signatures of approval; documentation of the nature and extent of review procedures performed; logs or memoranda relative to questions, exceptions and rejections; and other evidence) by the parties concerned. A list of these parties might include:

(a) For technical considerations: the architect/engineer, the owner's project manager, and the construction manager.

(b) For financial, tax, and accounting considerations: the comptroller, budget director, or internal auditor.

(c) For conformity to owner's project objectives: management.

2. Explosions have been compared to the original milestone schedule to assess their accuracy (comparing as appropriate, the milestone schedule to the explosions).

D. Reviewing (if appropriate), the documentation of EDP programs to evaluate the effectiveness with which programmed procedures relating to the preparation of construction schedules are functioning.

E. Reviewing "work" paths on explosions of dates to determine whether there are any conditions not properly considered in the past in determining scheduling that could have a significant effect on date explosions, such as bidder's or contractor's imminent bankruptcy, strikes, or forecasted inclement weather.

F. Assessing the extent to which the results of the finance and accounting function's review of the explosions have been taken into consideration for developing or amending items such as cash-flow schedules, tax planning, and financing arrangements.

G. Reviewing information requirements for the scheduling function, and:

   1. Trying to evaluate completeness, reasonableness, and propriety of information requirements, including retrieval, and updating.

   2. Determining whether contractors and others who must provide information for the scheduling function are effectively informed of their reporting responsibilities and are prepared to execute those responsibilities.

H. Ascertaining whether scheduling policies and procedures have been reviewed and approved by management.

I. Examining scheduling policies and procedures for:

   1. Coverage of:

      (a) Contractor reporting requirements.

      (b) Tasks to be performed by appropriate individuals.

      (c) Actions to be taken to minimize schedule shortfalls.

   2. Logic and consistency.

Quality Control/Assurance

Objective

Evaluate quality control/assurance.

Tasks

Review quality control policies, procedures, and forms and assess their effectiveness in relation to the various activities to which they are applicable, and determine whether quality control measures have been approved by the appropriate parties.

> *Comment 1.* The level of quality control varies between projects. The project manager should determine the level desired for each project. (The term "quality assurance" is used herein to denote a level of supervision independent of persons performing quality control on a day-by-day basis.)

The review should involve (as appropriate):

A. Determining whether the quality control policies, procedures, and forms have been reviewed and approved by management.

B. Examining quality control policies and procedures directed toward the owner's personnel, for:

1. Identification of:

   (a) Operations for which special training may be necessary before construction starts, for example, welding.

   Comment 2. Special training in skills such as welding is especially important in an "open shop" situation. Unionized workers are normally accredited (trained and licensed) in the skills their jobs call for.

   (b) Construction techniques involving exceptional precision or delicacy in execution.

2. Provision for:

   (a) Inspections of materials and equipment:
   In the vendor's plant during manufacturing.
   On receipt.

   (b) Inspections of construction:
   Routine "in-line" inspections (by workers).
   Quality control inspections (by persons independent of a particular construction task).
   Quality assurance reviews and inspections (by a top-level authority independent of day-to-day construction activities).

   (c) Inspection and acceptance of completed structures or systems.

   (d) Documentation of inspections performed and of actions taken, by such means as:
   Inspection forms.

   Comment 3. The use of the computer to generate inspection forms at specified contractor payment points should be considered. This will allow project inspectors to concentrate their efforts on inspection instead of paperwork.

   Exception notices.
   Corrective action reports.

Systems, procedures, and assignments to ensure that exceptions are acted on.

C.   Examining quality control policies and procedures directed toward contractors for inclusion of the following:

1.   Criteria governing quality of performance.
2.   Instructions for completing compliance forms, including timing for submission of reports.
3.   Backlog controls over exceptions.
4.   Charge-back routines.

D.   Evaluating quality control forms and inspection reports to assess whether they enhance efficiency of quality control.

E.   Evaluating policies, procedures, and related compliance forms generally for logic and consistency.

Active Project Coordination

Objective

Evaluate the coordination between the parties with major responsibilities in connection with the project.

Tasks

Review the coordination function and determine whether it has been properly defined and assigned to a responsible party and whether these steps have been approved by the appropriate parties.

Comment 1.   The parties with major project responsibilities include the owner, the architect, the construction manager, the general contractor, and all other contractors. In many cases, the responsibility for acting as coordinator will be assigned to the owner's project manager.

The review should involve:

A.   Determining whether the qualifications of the coordinator have been reviewed and approved by the entire management team.

B.   Assessing the degree of prestige and influence inherent in the position of coordinator.

C. Determining whether the coordination function as defined (or understood) provides for the ready transmission of information to or from any functional department or project party to meet the needs of any other.

D. Reviewing minutes of meetings, the schedule of proposed meetings, housekeeping arrangements, and progress reports to assess the adequacy of project coordination.

Comment 2. One task of the project coordinator is to identify factors which imperil project performance in a timely manner to contain negative impacts. For example, assume delay in delivery of a critical item; such a condition is likely to give rise to claims by contractors. The coordinator should (1) see to expediting and (2) minimize possible damage to contractors, and the size of the claims, by suggesting a series of alternatives for regaining the lost time.

CHAPTER SEVEN

Management Information System

INTRODUCTION

Strictly speaking, some form of management information system exists wherever management is carried on. As used today, however, the term "management information system" (MIS) connotes an ensemble of mechanisms and defined procedures for storing, retrieving, and distributing information. In any large construction project (and in most medium-sized ones) this formalized system is indispensable for project planning and implementation as well as for monitoring performance.

A successful management information system must have the following five characteristics:

Relevance. An MIS must serve the needs of the users at all levels of management concerned with the project (including the project and functional managers) and must be able to accommodate to exceptional situations.

Timeliness. The system must be able to deliver the information quickly.

Reliability. The information must be accurate.

Flexibility. The MIS must be adaptable to different phases of the project and able to accommodate exceptional or unexpected data.

Economy. The system must not cost more than it is worth.

OBJECTIVES AND TASKS

Design and Implementation Responsibilities Assigned

Objective

Determine whether the responsibilities for design and implementation of the MIS have been defined and assigned.

Tasks

Review the definition and assignment of responsibilities for design and implementation of MIS to determine whether they have been approved by the appropriate parties and whether the responsibilities address all significant tasks. The review should include:

A. Inquiring of systems personnel to ascertain whether the procedures performed (and the resulting reports, documents and recommendations) appear to be complete and appropriate.

B. Determining whether management has reviewed and approved the definition of responsibilities for design and implementation, as well as the actual assignment of those responsibilities.

C. Reviewing the defined responsibilities for coverage of:

1. System design, as evidenced by:
    (a) Provision for identification or definition of user needs (including functions outside of construction, such as accounting and finance).
    (b) Preparation of a clear statement of requirements to satisfy user needs.
    (c) Development of system specifications.
    (d) Translation of specifications into procedural, programming, and hardware specifications.
    (e) Implementation timetable.
    (f) Approach to selection of software and hardware.
    (g) Contractual arrangements with software and hardware vendors.

2. Implementation of the new system, as evidenced by:
    (a) Programming and program testing.
    (b) Development of system interfaces, as appropriate.
    (c) Data conversion and verification.
    (d) System testing.
    (e) System conversion preparation, if appropriate.
    (f) System installation.
3. Post-implementation, as evidenced by:
    (a) Review of administrative operations.
    (b) Identification of problem areas, determination of problem causes, and preparation of recommendations for solutions.
    (c) Documentation of system operating costs.
    (d) Evaluation of system performance and application of diagnostic techniques.
    (e) Training in system use and modification.

Solicitation of User Views

Objective

Evaluate the thoroughness with which user needs have been identified, assuming a measure of guidance to those users in formulating their views.

Tasks

Review documentation identifying user needs to determine whether the list has been reviewed and approved by the appropriate parties, and evaluate the list for completeness. The review and evaluation should involve:

A. Inquiring of persons performing, reviewing, and approving the assessment of user needs to ascertain whether the procedures performed (and the resulting reports, documents, and recommendations) appear to be complete and appropriate.
B. Determining whether reports documenting user needs as diagnosed have been reviewed and approved by persons exercising responsibility in appropriate functional departments.

C. Examining reports documenting user needs and information and reporting requirements from user departments for coverage of the following user requirements (as appropriate, in light of the nature and size of the project):

1. Planning and budgeting, as evidenced by:
   (a) Monitoring of results against performance measurement criteria, including incentives.
   (b) Performance appraisal.
   (c) Legal and regulatory compliance control.
   (d) Risk management control.
   (e) Explosion of the milestone schedule into a detailed construction schedule.
   (f) Incorporation of, or coordination with, the budget, scheduling system, and financing system.

2. Contract administration.

3. Affirmative action, as evidenced by minority business enterprise participation and minority work force compliance.

4. Claims processing.

5. Performance monitoring, as evidenced by:
   (a) Monitoring compliance with contract terms.
   (b) Monitoring performance in terms of cost, timeliness, and quality.

6. Materials management, as evidenced by:
   (a) Procurement.
   (b) Warehousing and inventory control.
   (c) Expediting.

7. Accounting and finance, as evidenced by:
   (a) A chart of accounts for fixed-asset accounting.

   Comment. The chart of accounts should not be so cumbersome that it is difficult to use. In addition, the chart should be consistent with responsibilities assigned to the accounting, procurement, estimating, and any other applicable functions.

   (b) Internal accounting controls.

(c) Federal Energy Regulatory Commission (FERC), EPA, and other federal and state accounting classifications, if appropriate.

(d) Federal, state, and local taxation and the opportunities to mitigate that taxation offered by tax regulations (i.e., investment tax credits, federal and state energy credits, job development credits, exemption or mitigation of sales use, and real and personal property taxes, etc.)

(e) Other cost-saving opportunities (for example, identification of vendors that give cash discounts or render "free," that is "bundled," ancillary services.)

8. Comprehensive coverage by MIS of functional MIS-served departments, individuals, or other entities—emphasizing the need for systems which can communicate—including:

(a) The owner.

(b) The construction manager.

(c) The general contractor.

(d) The architect.

(e) Others, if appropriate.

D. Assessing in a general way the reasonableness and propriety of identified requirements.

User Needs and Security Aspects Reflected in Specifications

Objective

Determine whether the MIS specifications cover user needs and security aspects.

Tasks

Check the MIS specifications to determine whether they have been reviewed and approved by the appropriate parties and include all identified user requirements. The review should involve:

A. Determining whether the MIS specifications have been reviewed and approved by the person responsible for MIS design and implementation.

B. Examining system technical specifications for coverage of:

1. Atmospheric requirements, essentially computer room temperature.
2. Space requirements.
3. Security of data and data access.
4. Security of the installation, backup, and "graceful degradation" (i.e., protection of program and data files during system shutdown after an unanticipated event, such as power or air conditioning failure).

C. Assessing in a general way MIS performance specifications in terms of:

1. Completeness (i.e., coverage of all user requirements).
2. Accuracy.
3. Timeliness.
4. Actionability (i.e., serviceability in determining whether action is to be taken).

Program Changes Subject to Security

Objective

Evaluate the system for initiating and approving program modifications.

Tasks

Review the procedures for introducing system modifications to determine whether modifications are to be approved by the appropriate parties and will be carried through. The review should involve:

A. Evaluating procedures for insuring that all necessary system modifications are identified.

B. Reviewing follow-up procedures on necessary modifications that are not made.

C. Ascertaining whether:

1. All system modifications have been reviewed and approved by both the user and the MIS departments.
2. The results of program testing have been reviewed and approved by appropriate MIS supervisory personnel.

    D.   Interviewing personnel and observing procedures to determine whether persons other than the programmers either performed or approved the test results.

    E.   As appropriate, reviewing test results and retesting (either by reperforming original procedures or by independent testing) to evaluate the effectiveness of system modifications.

Cost-Effective Software Acquisitions

Objective

Determine whether alternative approaches to procurement of software have been adequately explored.

Tasks

Review recommendations concerning whether to create software or buy it to determine whether recommendations have been approved by the appropriate parties, and evaluate the related research.

    Comment.   The usual choices are: (1) purchase of an existing system "as is"; (2) use of the construction manager's or general contractor's existing software; (3) purchase of a modular system subject to modifications or melding with custom-designed components; (4) design of a new system. It may be desirable to recruit skilled EDP systems analyst/programmers to facilitate adaptations of packages. It could also be advantageous to purchase an existing package with minimal modifications.

    The construction manager should play a key role in systems selection; an experienced construction manager is likely to have worked with a system he feels comfortable with.

The review and evaluation should involve:

    A.   Inquiring of persons performing, reviewing, and approving the completion of software selection to ascertain whether the procedures performed (and the resulting reports, documents, and recommendations) appear to be complete and appropriate.

    B.   Determining whether the final software recommendation has been reviewed and approved by MIS and project management.

C. Examining documents supporting the software recommendation, for inclusion of:

1. An estimate by an in-house or external expert of the cost of programming the construction system "from scratch" (taking into account hours and labor rates).

2. Estimates covering the cost of buying various software packages and adapting them to project needs.

3. The results of criteria or of tests applied to packages.

D. Trying to assess the validity of:

1. Labor-hour estimates, by reviewing (when appropriate) such factors as:

    (a) In-house or consultant programming capabilities and the amount of programming required.

    (b) Available packages, comparing them (with full regard to modifications that might be necessary) to in-house or consultant capabilities.

    (c) Proposals from software houses.

2. Labor rates, in light of:

    (a) Published rates.

    (b) Conditions that could significantly affect rates, such as labor contract renegotiation.

3. The software recommendation.

E. Reviewing the contract with the software house prior to signing it for such factors as reasonableness of controls, references, and likelihood of performance, and checking the contract provisions against the results of research and evaluation.

Item. A draft software contract did not prescribe a time-frame for delivery, did not specify which key contractor employees were to be assigned to the project, and did not cap software costs. Before the contract was signed, these deficiencies were remedied.

Cost-Effective Hardware Procurement

Objective

Determine whether alternative approaches to procurement of hardware and peripheral equipment have been adequately explored.

Tasks

Review the recommendation concerning procurement/leasing of hardware and peripheral equipment to determine whether it has been reviewed and approved by the appropriate parties, and evaluate the related research. The review and evaluation should involve:

A. Inquiring of persons performing, reviewing, and approving hardware acquisition to ascertain whether the procedures performed (and the resulting reports, documents, and recommendations) appear to be complete and appropriate.

B. Determining whether the hardware/peripheral equipment procurement recommendation has been reviewed and approved by both MIS and project management.

C. Examining documents supporting the procurement recommendation, for inclusion of:
   1. Specifications covering processing capabilities and capacities of hardware/peripherals under consideration.
   2. Atmospheric requirements for hardware.
   3. An overall ranking of hardware based on capability and capacity, atmospheric requirements, and price.

D. Evaluating hardware procurement research:
   1. By at least one of the following steps:
      (a) Reviewing results of tested capabilities and atmospheric requirements.
      (b) Querying other companies or outside consultants about their knowledge of capabilities, atmospheric requirements, frequency and timeliness of repair records, and other factors.
   2. Examining documents supporting the method of procuring hardware/peripherals:
      (a) For coverage of the following alternatives:
      Purchase, with consideration of:
      Financing costs (i.e., the present value of cash outlay).
      The residual value of the equipment at end of construction.

The usability of the computer after construction is completed, with attention to such factors as the likelihood of other construction projects being undertaken, the adaptability of existing software to the hardware under consideration, and the nature and extent of projected processing requirements in general.

Lease, with consideration of:

Financing costs (i.e., the present value of the cash outlay).

The advantages of month-to-month versus fixed-term leases.

Use of service center, with consideration of:

The present value of processing costs.

The location of the center (for turn-around considerations).

(b) To assess:

The reasonableness of interest rates used in the lease-versus-buy calculations (for example, by reference to the prime rate and to implicit rates as confirmed by lessors).

The propriety of cash flows (i.e., by reference to lease or purchase agreements).

3. Trying to determine whether any conditions exist that contradict (or seriously qualify) the conclusions of the procurement research, for example, discontinuance of a hardware product line or introduction of new equipment that is both better and less expensive than existing models.

Security in the Computer Facility

Objective

Evaluate the security aspects of MIS policies and procedures.

Tasks

Examine the MIS policies and procedures to determine whether they have been reviewed and approved by the appropriate parties, and evaluate the security scope of the policies and procedures. The review and evaluation should involve:

A. Determining whether MIS policies and procedures have been reviewed and approved by the person responsible for MIS design and implementation, and by management.

B. Examining policies and procedures:
1. For coverage of the following points:
   (a) Of a general nature:
      Objectives of the policies.
      Responsibilities and authority associated with each MIS function.
   (b) Pertaining to operations:
      Program modifications.
      Procedures governing:
         Computer room access.
         Loading and running programs.
         Documentation of computer usage.
         Protection of data.
         Operation of the library.
         Computer room emergencies, especially provision of "graceful degradation," backup facilities, and off-site data storage.
   (c) Pertaining to personnel:
      Duties associated with all positions in the MIS organizational structure, including performance measurement criteria.
      Evaluation of job applicants.
      Labor utilization, especially in regard to:
         Rotations among jobs and shifts.
         Required vacations.
         Instant termination.
         Training.
2. For logic and consistency.

Systems Personnel Trained in the State of the Art

Objective

Evaluate the staffing and training of MIS personnel.

Tasks

Review documentation relative to hiring and termination practices and training of MIS personnel to determine whether staff qualifications have been properly evaluated and whether the staff is receiving adequate training. The review should involve:

A.   Examining recommendations to hire to determine whether they have been reviewed and approved by responsible officials and whether the reasons supporting the recommendations are documented.

B.   Examining personnel files to determine whether they provide for:
    1.   Verification of qualifications (i.e., checks of references, employment and education records, and other qualifications).   .
    2.   Rotation of duties.
    3.   Issuance of access devices and exaction from employees of written commitments to comply with rules.
    4.   Instant termination policy.

C.   Reviewing the MIS training program.

Systems Documented

Objectives

Evaluate systems documentation.

Tasks

Review the systems manual, flow charts, and operating procedures to determine whether they have been approved by the appropriate parties and accurately reflect programs, data files, and other essentials. The review should involve:

A.   Determining whether the systems manual, systems flow charts, and operating procedures have been reviewed and approved by the person(s) responsible for systems design and implementation.

B.   Examining documents:
1.   To assess their accuracy by comparing them to actual programs and systems software.
2.   For coverage of the following (if appropriate):
(a)   Input application control procedures, regardless of whether data input takes place at only one centralized location or at several (i.e., through use of terminals on site).
(b)   Controls for editing rejected data and for its resubmission.
(c)   Controls to ensure continued and proper operation of programmed procedures.
3.   For logical arrangement, clarity, and effectiveness as communications tools.

Control over Data Accuracy and Completeness

Objective

Evaluate the functioning of internal accounting controls.

Tasks

Review the system of environmental and application controls built into the management information system to evaluate data security and audit trails. The review and evaluation should involve:

A.   Determining whether the system includes:
1.   Controls over program security, computer operations, and data security.
2.   Application controls over data for:
(a)   Completeness of input and update.
(b)   Accuracy of input and update.
(c)   Authorization of input and update.

B.   Appraising the effect of controls on the operational efficiency of the MIS system, with a view toward identifying redundant or unnecessary controls.

Interactive Systems, That is, Systems Capable of "Talking to Each Other"

Objective

Evaluate the systems interfaces between the construction MIS and related systems (for example, those of the owner and the architect or the construction manager/general contractor).

Tasks

Review interfaces, with special attention to the way in which they were developed and tested. The review should involve:

A. Examining relevant MIS documentation to determine whether all significant interfaces between the construction MIS and other systems (such as those of the architect/engineer, or the construction manager/general contractor) have been properly developed.

B. Determining whether interface requirements have been evaluated by construction MIS personnel and personnel representing interactive systems and that agreement exists as to the manner of interaction.

C. Trying to assess the effectiveness of interface software (i.e., by analysis and evaluation of software, and by reviewing the results of independent testing).

D. Evaluating, on the basis of information obtained from owner policies and procedures and by interviewing owner personnel and (when appropriate) observing:

   1. The completeness, accuracy, and validity of all data transmitted to the other systems.
   2. The safeguarding of data during transmission from one system to another.

Preoperational Tests

Objective

Determine whether adequate preoperational testing is performed prior to systems acceptance.

Tasks

Review documentation of preoperational tests and determine whether all appropriate parties will review and approve processing and whether the MIS department is to review and approve programmed procedures. The review should involve:

A.   Inquiring of persons performing, reviewing, and approving the test arrangements to ascertain whether the procedures performed (and the resulting reports, documents, and recommendations) appear to be complete and appropriate.

B.   Determining whether:

    1.   All user departments have reviewed and approved output from the MIS department for conformity to their requirements, as well as for logical arrangement and clarity.

    2.   The person responsible for the MIS implementation is to review and approve the results of preoperational testing of programmed procedures (on the basis of signatures of approval, documentation of the nature and extent of review procedures performed, and memoranda relative to questions).

C.   Determining, by examination of evidence and if necessary by interviewing personnel and observing procedures directly, whether pre- and post-operational testing is to be performed or approved by persons other than programmers involved in programming the application tested.

D.   Assessing testing and the results obtained (possibly involving test reperformance, and analysis of test programs).

CHAPTER EIGHT

Contract Administration

INTRODUCTION

Contract administration is related to the construction supervisory function; contract administrators work closely with the construction staff and with contract administrators assigned to field offices. Sometimes contract administration is included as a function and element of the general superintendent's office, which then assumes both a supervisory and administrative role. The contract administration function may be conducted partially or entirely from the procurement office or from a special office.

Contract administration can embrace a spectrum of management activities. In this discussion, we focus on two: contracting and progress evaluation. Closely related to these activities are control of change-orders and handling of contractor payment requests. Contract administration services, all except the last two, performed prior to construction, include, but are not restricted to:

1. Developing standard contract and contract policies.
2. Conducting bid "packaging," prequalifying prospective bidders, and soliciting bid invitations.
3. Conducting prebid conferences and visits to the job site.
4. Evaluating bids, proposed work schedules, and bidders' qualifications.
5. Conducting preaward conferences.
6. Recommending awards.
7. Conducting preconstruction conferences.

8. Evaluating the progress of work in place and the extent to which materials have been delivered and incorporated in the construction (in the construction phase).
9. Maintaining the permanent file of contract documents (in the construction phase).

OBJECTIVES AND TASKS

Recognition of the Importance of Contract Administration

Objective

Evaluate the contract administration function's place in the organizational structure.

Tasks

Review the contract administration function (CAF) to determine whether (1) its organizational structure has been approved by the appropriate parties, (2) activities of the CAF are being reported to management, and (3) staff qualifications have been properly evaluated. The review should involve:

A. Determining whether the CAF organizational structure has been reviewed and approved by management.
B. Examining the CAF organizational structure:
    1. To determine whether there is a reporting line to one person on the management level responsible for the project.
    2. To evaluate the interrelationship with other functional departments.
C. Examining job descriptions to determine whether:
    1. They were reviewed and approved at appropriate levels of management.
    2. They embody adequate performance measurement criteria.
    3. They have been prepared for all positions.
D. Evaluating the size of the staff projected in light of planned activities.
E. Reviewing screening techniques for evaluation of applicants.

F. Examining recommendations for hiring to determine whether they have been reviewed and approved by management and whether the reasons supporting the recommendations are adequately documented.

G. Examining personnel files to determine whether they provide for verification of qualifications (i.e., by checks of references, employment, and education records, and other sources).

Comment. On some projects the owner may administer several contracts and the construction manager the remainder. In this case, both organizations must be reviewed and interface responsibilities defined.

Optimal "Shopping" Policies

Objective

Evaluate owner "shopping" and negotiating policies.

Tasks

Review policies to determine whether they have been approved by the appropriate parties and whether the policies adopted are optimal from the point of view of encouraging contractor performance and fostering cost-savings. The review should involve:

A. Inquiring of persons responsible for the development of contracting policies to ascertain whether the approaches, and the resulting procedures, adequately protect the owner's interest.

B. Determining whether:

1. Contract policies have been reviewed and approved by management.

2. An open or closed bidding system is (or is to be) used.

   Comment 1. Bidding systems can be classified as open or closed. In an open bid system, any company may bid on any given job as long as it meets criteria established in the bid solicitation. Owners utilizing an open system usually advertise for bids in trade magazines or newspapers; the owner generally cannot evaluate contractors until after the bids are received. In closed bidding, the owner prequalifies bidders and invites only a selected number of contractors to submit proposals. There is no public opening of proposals and the owner conducts the process more selectively and secretly than under the open bid system.

Open bidding generally calls for more detailed stipulations than closed bidding. Such matters as bonding, bid opening, the form of proposals, disqualification of bids, and compliance with technical specifications must be covered.

Open bidding is generally utilized where the project is owned by government; closed bidding is prevalent where ownership is private.

3. The dollar-value criteria for bidding, and the numbers of bids to be sought, are reasonable relative to the value and importance of the materials or services involved.

D. Examining contract policy recommendations to determine whether viable contract approaches have been identified and pros and cons evaluated; for example:

1. Lump-sum (with or without escalation clauses).

2. Cost-plus (fixed fee or a percentage of cost; with or without upper limit).

3. Unit price (with or without upper limit).

E. Determining whether contract policies:

1. Include appropriate cost-saving incentives and cost-increasing disincentives for contractors.

   Comment 2. Contractors should be given incentives to encourage superior performance and discourage poor performance. An example of an incentive is the right to share in savings; an example of a disincentive is a provision, in a unit-price contract, whereby unit prices are lowered if total units exceed an agreed-upon maximum. If contractors suggest contract targets, incentives, or caps (upper limits of owner obligation in cost-plus contracts), the arrangements should be approved by persons other than the contractor and others whose performance evaluation may be contingent on the achievement of the target.

2. Have been reviewed and approved by legal counsel, and, in his view, comply with applicable laws and afford the owner

adequate protection. In the process, legal counsel should be questioned as to the review procedures performed in arriving at his conclusion and, if necessary, asked for documentation.

3. Cover the following:

(a) Repetitive and emergency buying based on evaluation of alternative procurement approaches and coordination with other internal or external procurement activities, if appropriate.

(b) Spare parts procurement and inventory.

Comment 3. Procedures should expedite purchase and delivery of spare parts while minimizing investment. Among typical procurement policies are those calling for purchase of spare parts on the open market when the need arises (often based on a reorder point of zero) and purchase under contract with a supplier.

(c) Operating stores.

Comment 4. In many cases, integration of construction stores with operating stores can result in buying economies and can help reduce inventory investment.

F. Assessing the reasonableness and propriety of contract policies, emphasizing control and cost optimization.

Procedural Guidance

Objective

Evaluate contract administration policies and procedures.

Tasks

Review policies and procedures to determine whether they have been approved by the appropriate parties; evaluate the thoroughness with which responsibilities and tasks are defined. The review and evaluation should involve:

A. Determining whether the CAF policies and procedures have been reviewed and approved by management.

B.   Examining policies and procedures.

    1.   For coverage of the following:

       (a)   Objectives of the policies.

       (b)   Responsibilities and authority associated with contract administration function.

       (c)   Duties associated with all positions in the function's organizational structure (in the form of job descriptions).

       (d)   Criteria governing when a contract should be executed and when purchase orders should be issued.

       (e)   The type or types of contracts to be used (e.g., lump-sum, cost-plus, time and material, or unit price).

       (f)   Change-orders, specifically in regard to:

Accounting for the orders and "tracking" their status.

The responsibility for the research and evaluation required to determine whether proposed change-order work is within the scope of the original contract (in-scope) and therefore not a valid reason for a cost increase, or outside its scope (out-of-scope) and therefore a valid reason.

Comment 1.   If a change is deemed to be in-scope, payment should either not be made, or should be made under protest, with right of recovery explicitly reserved. (Protest notifications should be subject to accounting control, even though in practice payments made under protest are rarely recovered.) If a change is deemed to be out-of-scope, the reason should be disclosed and evaluated. If the change was the fault of another contractor, consideration should be given to action against the contractor. If part of the cost is to be borne by other agencies, a determination of cost-sharing should be made and billing initiated.

The responsibility for and the research required to derive cost estimates for change-orders.

The extent of required "shopping" for additional prices on change-orders and delegation of the requisite responsibility to a person with appropriate independence.

(g) Record-keeping requirements, especially requirements relative to claims management.

(h) Evaluation and approval of consultant contracts.

(i) Procurement/inventory management, specifically in regard to:

Repetitive and emergency buying.

Spare parts procurement and inventory.

Operating stores.

Comment 2. Procurement of materials may be the responsibility of the construction contractors. In many cases, however, the owner has the capability to perform this function effectively. Therefore, consideration should be given to the cost-effectiveness of owner procurement versus contractor procurement.

(j) Bidding and contractor selection, including prequalification.

(k) Contractor performance evaluation.

2. Reasonableness and propriety.

3. Logic and consistency.

"Stand Alone" Bid Packages

Objective

Evaluate a sample or prototype bid package.

Comment 1. The bid package represents the standard information given to prospective bidders. Its main elements are: (1) general stipulations designed to protect the owner's interest; (2) special conditions that are usually specific to the contract or the project; (3) the "pro forma contract," which alerts vendors to what is desired; (4) the "form of proposal," which instructs prospective bidders how to submit price data; (5) instructions to bidders, containing such data as bid due date, number of proposal copies required, where questions should be directed, the date of the prebid meeting, how and when to visit sites, the type of bids desired, and schedule requirements; (6) rules for preparation of technical specifications and drawings.

Tasks

Review the standard bid package to determine whether it has been reviewed and approved by the appropriate parties and whether the stipulations in the package give a reasonable number of bidders a fair chance to bid competitively while safeguarding the owner's interest. The review should involve:

A. Determining whether the following have reviewed and approved the standard bid package and that their comments have been considered by a qualified party and incorporated into the package where feasible:

1. The project (or construction) manager, general contractor, architect, or engineer, for conformity to technical specifications and schedule and qualitative considerations.

2. The general counsel (or outside counsel), for compliance with laws; inclusion and wording of clauses covering damage, arbitration, affirmative action and minority business enterprise guidelines; and other matters with legal implications.

3. The general counsel (or director for environmental licensing), for identification of pertinent federal, state, and local requirements.

4. A financial officer, in connection with finance, tax, budgeting, and accounting considerations.

5. The insurance manager, in connection with risk management and risk reduction (the latter through safety and loss control measures) relating to both construction and operations.

6. The construction manager (if available), for compliance with site work rules and regulations and compatibility with the work of other contractors and in connection with contract administration.

   Comment 2. Bid packages are often composed of input from several parties, especially the owner, the architect or engineer, and the construction manager. One party should be designated as responsible for assembling the presentation, resolving conflicts, and filling gaps.

B. Examining the bid package for:

1. Coverage of the following:

   (a) General matters:

   A definition of specific work.

A contractual definition of the scope of the work.

Change-order requirements.

The control posture of the owner.

Timetables of key dates to be achieved.

A "time is of the essence" clause.

Billing procedures.

Requirements for measurement, payment, and any related procedures (in clear, well-defined terms).

Reporting requirements in terms of physical progress.

> *Comment 3.*   Contractor reporting requirements should be detailed enough to enable the client to monitor performance, but not so detailed that they impede progress. Having the contractor complete forms generated by the construction MIS may promote timeliness.

Routines to be followed for engineering changes (those exceeding scope as well as those within scope) and specifically the manner of determining prices and of affecting schedule changes.

Contractor supervision requirements including résumés of key executives.

Contractor's guarantees.

Compliance with laws.

Compliance with affirmative action and minority business enterprise guidelines.

Responsibility for damages.

Inspection and acceptance.

Arbitration and liquidated damages.

The owner's right to do work.

Termination and suspension rights.

Quality control/assurance.

Licensing requirements.

Cooperation between contractors.

Safety programs.

Supply of temporary facilities, such as office space and utilities.

Site security.

Line and grade control.

Grievance procedures.

Patent rights.

Contractor housekeeping.

(b) Accounting and financial matters:

The right to demand audits and the responsibility for absorbing audit costs.

Accounting records required to be kept by the contractors.

Progress payments.

Retention provisions and release.

Contractor's credit.

Insurance requirements.

Bid, performance, and payment bond requirements.

(c) Features that make for operational savings and efficiency such as:

Shared incentives for superior performance and disincentives for poor performance.

Standardization of materials to reduce procurement costs.

Value analysis.

Comment 4. Value analysis (sometimes called value engineering) is performed to minimize life-cycle costs. For instance, if the unit price of sawblade A is half that of sawblade B but sawblade B lasts four times as long, sawblade B is the better value.

Wrap-up insurance, cash-flow plans, and loss control programs.

2. Logic and consistency.

Effective Distribution of Bid Packages

Objective

Evaluate bid packages for completeness and determine whether each has received appropriate review and approval.

Tasks

Review individual bid packages to determine whether they have been approved by appropriate parties prior to sending out and include all appropriate standard and nonstandard provisions.

> *Comment.* It is important that the packages reflect all authorized deviations from the standard contract, but no unauthorized ones.

The review should involve:

A. Examining correspondence to determine whether the following have reviewed and approved each bid package prior to sending out invitations to bid:

1. The project manager (construction manager, architect, or engineer), for conformity to technical specifications.

2. The general counsel (or outside counsel), for compliance with laws; inclusion and wording of clauses covering damage, arbitration, affirmative action and minority business enterprise guidelines, and other matters with legal implications.

> *Item.* In connection with the construction of a steam generating station we reviewed the draft of a $150,000,000 balance-of-plant contract. Some 80 provisions were inserted to protect the owner's interest. In this way, certain aspects of risk were shifted to the balance-of-plant contractor.

3. The construction manager (if available), for compliance with site work rules and regulations and compatibility with the work of other contractors and in connection with matters pertinent to contract administration.

4. The general counsel (or director for environmental licensing), for identification of pertinent federal, state, and local requirements to be complied with.

5. The financial officer, in connection with finance, tax, and accounting considerations.

6. The insurance manager, in connection with risk coverage and risk reduction (the latter through safety and loss control measures) relating to both construction and operations.

B. Endeavoring to assess the requirements in the bid package for balance, i.e., being sufficiently stringent to discourage change-orders and claims, yet not so stringent as to discourage bidders and raise the dollar level of bids received.

CHAPTER NINE

Contractor Selection

INTRODUCTION

The usual method of selecting contractors is by inviting and processing bids (see "Shopping Policies," Comment 1). Selection by other methods may be practical in certain circumstances; for example, when the capabilities of the contractor are thought to be unique, bidding may be bypassed. However, it must be kept in mind that bidding may be mandated on government-owned or supported projects. Indeed, in some states, even the nature of prime contracts may be prescribed by law for government-owned projects. (Closed bidding may also run afoul of legal obstacles.)

Bidding is carried out in three stages: first, solicitation of bids; second, receipt and evaluation of the bids; and third, award of the contract. The procedures connected with these three main phases should be made known to prospective bidders. The bidding plan is prepared by the owner's staff or sometimes by the construction manager. The procedures detailed in the plan should be followed meticulously, because deviations from them could be construed as favoritism or caprice and give rise to civil actions.

Notwithstanding the necessary dependence on a prepared syllabus of procedures, the process of contractor selection is more judgmental than mechanical. It must be entrusted to persons who are familiar with bid strategy, types of contracts, confidentiality of procedures, evaluation of qualified bidders, and other aspects.

OBJECTIVES AND TASKS

Owner-Protective Bidding

Objective

Evaluate procedures involving bidding and other means of contractor selection.

Tasks

Review bidding procedures to determine whether they have been approved by the appropriate parties and give a reasonable number of bidders a fair chance to bid competitively, while safeguarding the owner's interest; alternative routines should be specified when competitive bidding is not advisable or feasible. The review should involve:

A. Inquiring of persons performing, reviewing, and approving contractor/vendor selection to ascertain whether the procedures performed (and the resulting reports, documents, and recommendations) appear to be complete and appropriate.

B. Determining whether bidding procedures:
1. Have been approved by decision-makers.
2. Call for:
    (a) A minimum dollar value for competitive bidding.
    (b) Notification to potential bidders.
    (c) A prebid conference.
    (d) In closed bidding, a method of inviting bidders.

    Comment. A common practice in connection with closed bidding is to utilize a list of contractors and vendors whose qualifications have been determined, that is, who are *prequalified.* The list may reflect previous experience as well as preference in favor of local firms. The list should be evaluated by reference to any files that the owner may have compiled on previous or potential contractor contacts.
3. Have been reviewed and approved by legal counsel for compliance.

C. Determining whether effective provision is made for alternative procedures when competitive bidding is not advisable or feasible.

D. Reviewing bidding procedures generally for logic and consistency.

Bidder Prequalification Where Possible

Objective

When closed bidding is permitted, evaluate the method by which potential bidders are prequalified.

Tasks

Review documentation of the vendor qualification process to determine whether only vendors with the requisite technical capability (as evidenced by personnel, facilities, and other specifics) and financial capability are invited to submit bids. The review should involve:

A. Determining whether the consensus to qualify or reject a potential bidder is to be reviewed and approved by management and legal counsel.

Comment 1. Consensus recommendations are standard in larger operations because of the difficulty in achieving true unanimity, different supporting reviews having as a rule differing evaluation criteria. Consensus recommendations should include documented consideration of and reasons for not agreeing with dissenting opinion(s).

B. Reviewing the investigation of contractor qualifications to determine whether the following qualifications are to be documented for each contractor:

1. Technical capability.

2. Satisfactory performance history in terms of cost, timeliness, and quality (as determined on the basis of past performance, on similar-type contracts).

3. Adequate warehousing and distribution facilities (as determined by direct inspection, where appropriate).

4. Financial soundness (as determined by inspection of audited financial statements, credit ratings, and reports).

5. Satisfactory references.

6. Adequate provision for supervisory staff (as determined on the basis of proposed staffing arrangements and personnel qualifications).

7. Sufficient freedom from other commitments (as determined by reference to specific lists of such commitments).

8. Posting of appropriate bonds in connection with bidding, performance, and payment.

   Comment 2. In the open bidding process, a low bidder may in many cases not be refused award even if unfavorable information is on file. In the closed bidding process, the discretionary latitude for disqualification is much wider; nonetheless, consultation with legal counsel is advisable.

C. Reviewing supporting documents in an effort to evaluate the reasonableness of the decisions to prequalify or reject bidders.

D. Assessing whether any information exists that contradicts or modifies conclusions about the acceptability of a contractor for consideration under closed bidding.

Broad Bid Solicitation

Objective

Determine whether the client has given a reasonable number of bidders an opportunity to bid.

Tasks

Review documentation dealing with the number of "invited bidders" and with the criteria by which they were selected. The review should involve:

A. Reviewing notification procedures to potential bidders for coverage of:

1. Methods of notification.

   Comment 1. If an open bid system is used, the focus should be on whether there was adequate advertising and on whether a sufficient number of contractors was given the opportunity to bid.

2. Prequalification requirements (if prequalification is permissible by law).

B. Reviewing, and if appropriate, observing the procedures followed in prebid conferences, specifically:

1. Agendas and minutes, for evidence of review and approval by project managers.

2. Agendas, for evidence that:

    (a) All significant items in bid packages were fully explained.

    (b) Opportunities were granted to potential bidders to comment on bid packages and make suggestions for improvement.

    Comment 3. Suggestions from potential bidders may, at times, identify viable alternatives to bid package specifications.

3. Minutes for:

    (a) Names of all attendees (for later comparison to list of actual bidders).

    (b) Items discussed and questions raised.

    Comment 3. Contractor's questions are often answered formally in the minutes. These minutes usually become a part of the later contract. Prebid meeting minutes should be distributed to all concerned, including bidders, project manager, construction manager, architect/engineer, and legal counsel. Besides reviewing the minutes themselves, the owner should review their distribution.

C. If prequalification of bidders is permissible by law, reviewing procedures for selecting invited bidders from among those prequalified (for example, elimination of all out-of-state bidders):

1. To determine whether the selection of invited bidders has been reviewed and approved by management and legal counsel, if appropriate.

2. To observe bidder selection to evaluate compliance with procedures and essential fairness.

D. Examining the list of invited bidders to see which have accepted invitations to bid and if there were any abstainers:

1. To determine whether reasons were sought in each case.

    2. If appropriate, to review the selection process for replacement bidders.

E. Reviewing and observing directly, if appropriate, sealed bid procedures, including bid openings, to ascertain whether:

    1. Bids are received unopened by a responsible person (independent of contract awards and accounts payable) and are dated and time stamped under that person's control.

    2. If the open bidding system is used, bidders may have more than one envelope.

        Comment 4. Bidders may reserve their options in regard to the amount bid until they are able to exercise them on the basis of the perceived level of competition. This is done by preparing envelopes with different amounts. If it is obvious that little competition exists and that bidders have more than one envelope, rebidding or even a re-evaluation of the feasibility of bidding on that contract may be appropriate.

    3. Bids and the sealed engineer's estimate were opened publicly.

Objective Bid Evaluation

Objective

Evaluate the procedures that exist to ensure that bids are properly considered.

Tasks

Review the documentation of bid evaluation procedures to determine whether each bid is to be reviewed for conformity to specifications and placed on a common evaluation basis and whether an expressed and approved consensus will exist as to the recommended low bidder.

    Comment 1. Often, bids do not conform exactly to bid package specifications; for example, a contractor may enter modifications which could, at times, represent viable alternatives. When this happens, an attempt should be made in the bid evaluation process to account for these modifications in order to keep all bidders on as close to an equal footing as possible. If this is not feasible, rebidding may be necessary.

The review should involve:

A. Determining whether the consensus recommendation bidder will be reviewed and approved by management (as evidenced by signatures of approval, documentation of the nature and extent of review procedures performed, and logs or memoranda recording questions, exceptions, and rejections).

Comment 2. As noted, recommendations based on consensus may be standard in larger operations because of the difficulty in achieving true unanimity (different supporting reviews having differing evaluation criteria). Consensus recommendations should include documented consideration of dissenting opinion(s).

B. Assessing the reasonableness of the consensus recommendation by reference to documented reasons and approved evaluations of all bids.

C. Examining the proposal of the apparent low bidder for clarity of meaning and conformance to the bid package.

D. Determining whether the completion of bid evaluation is to be reviewed and approved by appropriate supervisory and management personnel (often such parties are designated by a bid award committee).

Equitable Award Routines

Objective

Evaluate the function of the bid award committee.

Tasks

Review documents supporting creation, staffing, and authority of the bid award committee. The review should involve:

A. Inquiring of persons performing, reviewing, and approving bid awards to ascertain whether the procedures to be performed (and the resulting reports, documents, and recommendations) appear complete and appropriate.

    B. Determining whether the organizational structure of, and the authority given to, the bid award committee is to be reviewed and approved by management.

    C. Examining award procedures to determine whether they provide for:

       1. Consideration in the bid evaluation of the following:

          (a) Conformity of bids to specifications.

          (b) Vendor financial, technical, and supervisory capability (to the extent not determined in the prequalification process).

          (c) Historical performance with the owner and with other companies.

       2. Compiling all evaluations and recommending the apparent low bidder.

       3. Identifying and fully controlling matters remaining to be negotiated with the apparent low bidder.

       4. Approval of awards:

          (a) To other than the lowest bidder.

          (b) Where the number of bids is less than competitive.

          (c) Where affirmative action or minority business enterprise issues are involved.

Controlled Post-Bid Negotiations

Objective

Determine whether negotiations with the apparent low bidder are controlled to protect the owner's interest.

Tasks

Review documentation of negotiations with the apparent low bidder to identify any actual or potential concessions from the original bid package, and if there are any, determine whether steps are to be taken to minimize significant ill effects. The review should involve:

    A. Determining whether:

       1. Management is to review and approve the results of the negotiation process and will evaluate concessions affecting project cost, scheduling, and quality.

2.   Reviews designed to ensure that bids are responsive, and to place bidders on a common basis, are performed by:

(a)   The project manager (construction manager, engineer or architect), for conformity to technical specifications.

(b)   The financial officer, in connection with finance, tax, budgeting, and accounting considerations.

(c)   The general counsel (or outside counsel), for compliance with laws and for inclusion and wording of clauses covering damage, arbitration, affirmative action and minority business enterprise requirements, and other matters having to do with protecting the owner's legal position.

(d)   The insurance manager, in connection with insurance policies, bid, performance and payment bonds, funding arrangements, and risk reduction through safety and loss control programs.

B.   As appropriate, checking information in the bid evaluations by reference to sources and assessing the reliability of the sources.

C.   Considering whether there is any information not weighed in the bid evaluation that could significantly affect it.

D.   Assessing the adequacy and propriety of the review performed, with attention to the methods of documenting the bid evaluation process, especially the advisability of using standardized forms or checklists, or both (where not already in use).

Presigning Final Contract Review

Objective

Evaluate the final review applied to construction contracts before they are signed.

Tasks

Determine whether appropriate parties are to approve all construction contracts prior to signing. Review the contract provisions and the basis of contract awards to detect potential problems. The determination and review should involve:

A. Determining whether:

1. The final construction contract is to be reviewed and approved prior to execution by the following parties:

    (a) The project manager (construction manager, engineer or architect), for conformity to technical specifications.

    (b) The general counsel (or outside counsel), for compliance with laws and for inclusion and wording of clauses covering damage, arbitration, affirmative action and minority business enterprise requirements, and other matters having to do with protecting the owner's interests.

    Item. A public utility experienced a significant delay in starting construction of a major project. Accordingly, we were asked to review major open equipment purchase orders to determine which ought to be cancelled and rebid—incurring cancellation charges—and which ought to be continued, incurring escalation. In addition, we determined that there were some cases with respect to which deliveries should actually be stepped up to stop the running of escalation; for instance, despite high interest charges, a net saving of $500,000 was realized by early delivery of a cooling tower.

    (c) The general counsel (or director for environmental licensing), for identification of pertinent federal, state, and local requirements to be complied with within a suitable time frame.

    (d) The financial officer, in connection with finance, tax, budgeting, and accounting considerations.

    (e) The insurance manager, in connection with risk coverage and risk reduction (the latter through safety and loss control measures), relating to both construction and operation.

B. Checking the final contract against records of negotiations to ascertain whether all items subject to negotiation were properly taken into account.

C. If low bidder was not awarded the contract, determining whether the award was in accordance with applicable policies and procedures.

Controls over Consultants

Objective

Evaluate the method by which the need for consultants is determined and filled.

Tasks

Review contracts, as well as the research and analysis undertaken in preparing them, to determine whether they are receiving appropriate review at every stage.

> *Comment 1.* Because consultants deal with a wide variety of personal services, contracts with consultants are less amenable to standardization than vendor contracts. Some degree of standardization may be feasible, however, and is generally desirable.

The review should involve:

A. Determining whether the research and analysis performed as a basis for awarding a consultant contract have been reviewed and approved by management.

B. Evaluating the adequacy of the aforementioned research and analysis.

C. Assessing the adequacy and appropriateness of the procedures used to select a consultant, (i.e., requests for proposal, bidding, and award).

> *Comment 2.* In selecting consultants, it is generally to the owner's advantage to establish ground rules up front. Usually, owners will seek to strike a balance between selecting consultants on the basis of quality and selecting them on the basis of price; a one-for-four price/quality weighting arrangement is not unusual. Moreover, in the selection, greater emphasis is likely to be placed on the individual consultants proposed to be assigned to the engagement than on the general reputation of the consulting firm.

D. Determining whether contracts are to be reviewed prior to signing by:

1. The financial officer, in connection with accounting, tax, budgeting, payment terms, and related considerations.

2. The general counsel, for compliance with laws and for inclusion and wording of clauses covering damage, arbitration, affirmative action, minority business requirements, and other matters having to do with protecting the owner's interest.

3. Other functional department personnel, in connection with technical considerations, for example, deliverables and timing.

4. The insurance manager, if appropriate, in connection with required insurance.

5. Project managers, for conformity with overall project objectives.

E. Checking contract terms against:

1. Documented analysis to determine whether contract provisions reflect the findings of such analysis.

2. Budgets, if appropriate, to see whether consultant services are reasonably priced.

3. The construction schedule, if appropriate, to determine whether the consultant contract could impede construction progress.

Comment 3. Consultant contracts should specify what is to be delivered and within which time frame. Moreover, the value of services must be capped to avoid open-ended engagements. And, consultants' overhead allocations should be subject to audit; care should be taken in the contract to spell out which items are directly chargeable to the contract by the consultant, which items qualify as overhead, and which items cannot be passed on under any circumstances.

Item. Writing audit rights into contracts, and taking advantage of audit prerogatives, can be important particularly in the case of consulting contracts. With respect to one large Eastern city, construction consultants "loaded" overhead with such items as executive bonuses, EDP service charges (for systems not utilized) and prior period development costs, in violation of the rules of a cognizant federal agency. As a result of the auditor's report, steps were taken toward cost recovery.

Physical Control over Contract Documents

Objective

Determine whether all contract documents, together with any other contract information of value, are to be stored at an appropriate location.

Tasks

Review records of contract files for both home and field offices to determine whether all pertinent information is to be transferred to the group responsible for contract administration.

CHAPTER TEN

Affirmative Action

INTRODUCTION

Under a policy known as affirmative action, federal, state, and local governments impose requirements for employment of minorities, including minority-owned businesses, and women. The discussion in this section applies to affirmative action, minority business enterprises, and women's business enterprises. In some states the requirements are applicable only to publicly funded projects; on the federal level, they apply to all of a company's projects once federal affirmative action liability has been incurred for any project.

For some large companies, meeting the affirmative action requirements can entail additional actions—and expense. Large companies should be prepared to offer minority contractors continuous guidance and supervision in order to maintain basic standards of efficiency. (In certain states, companies are permitted a major role in setting their own affirmative action goals subject to official approval. To take full advantage of this privilege, a company might have to engage in considerable preparatory effort.)

The affirmative action program should be entrusted to a coordinator (or coordinating group) with interdepartmental authority over relations with minority enterprises.

OBJECTIVES AND TASKS

Compliance with Affirmative Action Rules

Objective

Evaluate the affirmative action function (AAF) for compliance with laws, and furtherance of company policies.

Tasks

Review the organizational structure of the AAF, its manpower authorization and specifications, and its policies and procedures to determine whether they are to be approved by the appropriate parties and comply with all federal or state guidelines and standards; assess the completeness of coverage of key points. The review and assessment should involve:

A. Inquiring of persons performing, reviewing, and approving affirmative action programs to ascertain whether the procedures to be performed (and the resulting reports, documents, and recommendations) appear to be accurate and complete.

B. Determining whether management has reviewed and approved:
1. The appointment of a coordinator.
2. The coordinator's job description.
3. The coordinator's manning table and manpower specifications.

   Comment.   If an individual coordinator has not been appointed, the objective may be accomplished by a committee.

4. Affirmative action policies and procedures.

C. Reviewing policies and procedures for:
1. Compliance with federal or state guidelines or standards, such as Public Law 95-512.
2. Coverage of the following points:
    (a) Objectives.
    (b) Responsibilities and authority associated with the AAF.
    (c) Duties of all positions in the organizational structure.
    (d) Setting of goals.

(e)   "Sourcing" of minority business enterprises and minority workers.

(f)   Minority business enterprise (MBE) certification.

(g)   MBE supervision and guidance.

(h)   Monitoring actual affirmative action activity against goals.

3.   Logic and consistency.

Meaningful Goals

Objective

Evaluate AAF targets and goals.

Tasks

Review AAF targets and goals to determine whether they are to be approved by the appropriate parties and appear reasonable.

Comment.   Goals may be set for employees in terms of the number of minority and women workers relative to the total. In addition, goals can be set in terms of the dollar value of contracts awarded, that is, the percentage that the total for MBEs is of all contracts awarded.

Generally, goals should involve an element of "stretch"; on the other hand, they should not be so idealistic as to be unrealistic, that is, leading to costs in excess of benefits, or heedless of the numbers of minority personnel available for employment.

The review should involve:

A.   Determining whether:

1.   The targets and goals set by the coordinator are to be approved by management.

2.   When the project is subject to federal or state and local affirmative action requirements—the goals are to be approved in writing by the proper governmental authorities.

B.   Assessing the reasonableness of the goals.

Accredited MBEs

Objective

Evaluate the system used for identifying MBEs and WBEs (Women's Business Enterprises).

Tasks

Review MBE identification and related procedures to determine whether certified MBEs are being identified.

Comment. Certification as an MBE is necessary before a contractor can be counted towards fulfilling the owner MBE goal. Many minority-owned businesses remain uncertified because they never requested certification. Where federal certification is needed, an award can be conditioned on the contractor's willingness to apply and on successful achievement of certification. (Where state regulation is involved, imposing such conditions may not be feasible given open bidding.) Where doubt exists, legal counsel should be consulted.

The review should involve:

A. Determining whether MBEs are to be certified by a federal or state agency when such certification is required.

Item. A cognizant federal agency decertified an alleged minority contractor. This resulted in delay of a $200 million project for approximately three months. If a timely effort had been made to check the potential minority contractor's financial status, supervisory capability, facilities, and performance record, the situation might have been averted.

B. Evaluating the scope and efficiency of efforts to locate eligible MBEs.

Item. A major transportation company was faced with the challenge of setting and achieving minority business enterprise and women's business enterprise goals in a sparsely populated area. We made recommendations relating to the "sourcing" of personnel, to identifying possible goal shortfalls, and to reporting accomplishments against targets.

C. Determining whether commitments were made by or to community organizations and if so, what kind, and whether the parties undertaking the commitments are being asked to fulfill them.

D. Where labor unions are signatory to an MBE plan, examining the appropriate commitment letters.

E. Determining whether any MBE certifications have been revoked, if so, why, and whether corrective action has been taken.

Evaluation of MBE Capabilities

Objective

Determine whether MBE capabilities and shortfalls are being evaluated effectively.

Tasks

Review documentation of MBE capabilities and shortfalls to determine whether they are being identified sufficiently well to enable management to provide proper guidance and supervision.

> *Comment.* Minority business enterprises are often on shakier financial and technical grounds than other contractors. Therefore early identification of shortfalls and focused supervision and guidance are often necessary. MBEs that are both certified and known to be competent are generally in great demand.

The review should involve:

A. Examining the following:
   1. MBE certifications.
   2. MBE qualifications, including financial condition, equipment, supervisory capacity, and shop capacity.
   3. Reports of inspections and interviews.
   4. Recommendations made by the affirmative action coordinator concerning special training, monitoring, and counseling, and determining whether the recommendations were followed up by the appropriate functional department.

Enhancing MBE Effectiveness

Objective

Evaluate procedures for supervision and guidance of MBEs and WBEs.

Tasks

Review MBE supervision and guidance procedures and documentation of supervision. The review should involve:

A. Examining MBE supervision and guidance procedures for coverage of:
    (a) Recommended actions (such as training and development) for correcting shortfalls.
    (b) Monitoring the MBE construction progress.
    (c) Reporting requirements.
    (d) Responsibilities for follow-up on findings.
B. Examining reports indicating observations, findings, and recommendations.

PART THREE

Compliance Phase

CHAPTER ELEVEN

Site Aspects

Site Security Observed

Objective

Evaluate measures taken for physical security at the construction site.

Tasks

Review policies and established procedures designed to promote security, determine whether they have been approved by the appropriate parties, and that they are being complied with. The review should involve:,

- **A.** Determining whether site security policies and procedures have been reviewed and approved by management.
- **B.** Visiting the site and inspecting arrangements indicative of:
    1. Passive surveillance, such as lighting, fencing, and alarm systems.
    2. Active surveillance, such as the presence of watchguards and trained dogs and the maintenance of sign-in procedures at security gates (the latter verifiable by direct observation as well as by inspection of sign-in sheets).

        Comment. Security measures should be in effect 24 hours a day, seven days a week.

        Item. In the case of an Eastern state, it was determined to be to the state's advantage to engage guards for a one-time major project by hiring a guard service. In this way the state did not incur the obligation of paying pensions and other employee benefits. However, given recurring construction situations, it may well be cost-effective to place guards on the owner's payroll.

3. Check-in routines, including maintenance of visitor logs and badge issuance and retrieval; check-out routines, including consideration of shipping authorizations, and truck and personal vehicle inspections.

4. Parking restrictions, including prohibitions against parking near storerooms.

5. Segregation in a secure area of items thought to be especially subject to pilferage, such as small hand tools, flashlight batteries, etc.

C. If security services are provided by an outside organization, reviewing the contract with that company to evaluate its services in relation to cost, with due consideration of make or buy implications.

Safety Rules Enforced

Objective

Evaluate the safety program.

Tasks

Review the safety program to determine whether it has been approved by the appropriate parties, is being complied with, and is functioning effectively. The review should involve:

A. Determining whether:

1. The safety program has been approved by top management.

2. The following have contributed to the development and initiation of the safety program: the construction manager; the general contractor; the labor unions, if appropriate; and other inside or outside parties with a valid interest in safety.

   Comment. Many insurance companies are now entering the field of industrial safety consulting; they may provide an owner resource.

B. Reviewing the safety program for:
    1. Provisions establishing rules and regulations for:
        (a) On-site safety.
        (b) Monitoring and processing of claims.
    2. Conformity with government requirements, particularly those of the Occupational Safety and Health Administration (OSHA).

C. Evaluating the functioning of operational and internal accounting controls, as discussed herein, with reliance on information obtained by questioning persons who perform the procedures and supervisors who approve that performance.

D. Reviewing reports on compliance with the safety program to determine whether they have been approved by appropriate management personnel. In this connection, attention should be given to recommendations by fire and other inspectors with a view to removing any qualifications which might move the owner into a specially rated category or into potential liability for fines.

Item. To the extent that safety violations involve OSHA, draconic fines may be imposed. However, even where the violations are discovered by fire inspectors, especially of mutual associations, alterations may be necessary to remove special assessments, penalties, or extra premiums. It may be less expensive to make modifications and restore preferred ratings than to incur add-on charges. In one case, construction of a fire wall valued at $200,000 removed add-on premiums amounting to $200,000 per annum—one-on-one cost recovery the first year!

E. Determining, by examining evidence, and if necessary by questioning personnel and observing procedures, whether safety program guidelines are being complied with.

F. Reviewing OSHA audit reports and any internal reports prepared in connection with OSHA requirements to evaluate the conformity of the project with such requirements.

G. Determining whether employee claims have been reviewed and approved by the appropriate management personnel and whether they have been given proper consideration, as evidenced by:
    1. Evaluation of claims for exposure.
    2. Actions taken to mitigate claims.

H. Reviewing the disposition of claims and evaluating the efficiency of the claims-processing function, on the basis of supporting documentation (such as injury reports, physicians' statements, and reports of investigations into causes of injuries).

I. Reviewing insurance policies and loss-experience data used to determine premiums to determine whether:

    1. Loss-experience data reflects only valid claims processed.

    Item. Where the constructor is in a position to pass unfavorable experience on to his customer, he lacks an incentive for loss control. Moreover, unscrupulous constructors have been known to organize their construction subsidiaries in such a manner as to "load" unwary owners with any unfavorable experience in a jurisdiction. In one such case, an auditor's questions resulted in reimbursement by the contractor of 20 percent of the total premiums involved.

    2. Premium billings can be supported by the insurance company (i.e., by analyzing claims processed, pending claims, loss reserves, and other data).

    3. The owner has exercised audit rights inherent in experience-rated policies (reviewing, if appropriate, the results of those audits).

    Item. A contractor billed the owner for workmen's compensation insurance at an estimated rate applied to direct labor. He was obligated to adjust that rate for actual experience. The owner sent an audit team to the insurance company with the result that the adjustment was expedited. Overall workmen's compensation insurance expense was reduced by 15 percent of $10 million.

J. Determining whether responsibilities for losses and claims are allocated to the appropriate parties and, specifically, whether contractors are bearing valid shares of cost as per contract terms.

K. Assessing the role of the insurance manager in monitoring safety and claims identification, evaluation, and processing.

Equipment Procurement and Temporary Facilities Comply with Contracts

Objective

Evaluate the methods used in procuring construction equipment and in managing temporary construction support facilities.

Tasks

Review (1) the procurement of construction equipment, to determine whether it is carried out in a cost-effective manner and has been reviewed and approved by appropriate parties, and (2) the construction and utilization of temporary construction support facilities, to determine whether these activities are properly managed and residual long-term benefits obtained from these facilities whenever possible.

Comment 1.   Construction, involving temporary support facilities, may be performed by craftsmen working directly for and supervised by the construction manager. This type of work is sometimes referred to as "force account" work to distinguish it from work subcontracted by the construction manager. Often force account work requires procurement of construction equipment. If so, the appropriate questions (such as make or buy, or rent or lease) should have been answered in arriving at a cost-effective acquisition. Caution is called for relative to equipment billed on the basis of its condition—such equipment should be secured in the *right* condition, but need not necessarily be brand-new. Incoming equipment inspection for conformity to the terms of the transaction is also necessary. Relative to unused equipment, contractors may rent such equipment to each other—the danger being that the owner is charged twice for the same equipment. It is necessary that equipment be kept busy while on site, and that it be removed when no longer required.

Item.   In one case involving a nuclear project, equipment was purchased for the project which became the property of the general contractor. After limited use—most of the equipment still looked new—the equipment was declared excess and sold at auction. At one such auction $5 million worth of equipment was sold at "bargain" prices. Further, the auction had not been advertised. The presumed loss to the owner approximated half the value of the equipment.

The reviews should involve:

A.   Determining whether:
1.   The construction equipment was procured on the basis of comprehensive analysis dealing with the alternatives of purchase, rent, or lease.
2.   The procurement method was approved by management.
B.   Determining, on the basis of information from contractors, whether temporary construction support facilities, such as those for security, fire protection, field office space, and utilities, are being provided in accordance with contract conditions.

> *Item.*   In planning security for a utility plant, a scale model was built for the facility including miniature fences, guard posts, roads, and gates. By manipulating the model, security officers were able to devise optimum protection at lowest possible cost. Physical modeling averted the erection and subsequent teardown of actual facilities and helped to achieve "more bang" for the security buck.

C.   Determining whether the responsibility for coordination and management of temporary construction support facilities is assigned to one party (usually the construction manager).

Comment 2.   If the responsibilities are assigned to each individual contractor, redundancies and additional costs are likely to result.

CHAPTER TWELVE

Drawings

Construction on Latest Approved Drawings

Objective

Evaluate control over project drawings.

Tasks

Review policies and procedures relative to drawings to determine whether they have been approved by the appropriate parties, are being complied with, and embody controls over the creation, approval, recording, safe keeping, and modification of drawings. The review should involve:

A. Determining whether policies and procedures relative to drawings have been reviewed and approved by management.

B. Examining policies and procedures relative to drawings for coverage of:

1. Control over creation (largely by the requirement for documentation of the need for a drawing).

2. Review and approval of drawings for technical correctness.

3. Distribution, through deliveries coordinated with construction schedules (especially with fast-track jobs).

    Comment 1. To the extent practicable, copies of drawings should be distributed only as the need arises. The greater the number of copies of drawings in circulation, the more difficult it is to control them and to retrieve superseded drawings.

139

4. Record keeping, through:

   (a) Proper designation for drawings in all stages.

   (b) Drawing numbering and sequencing.

   (c) Stamping to indicate drawing status (for example, "approved for construction," "issued for bid purposes only," or "preliminary").

   (d) Classification of drawings by function or by geographical area (for example, heating, ventilating, or air conditioning, or first floor, second floor, and so forth).

   (e) Identification of superseded drawings with a view towards destruction of unneeded copies.

   (f) Tracking requirements for drawings not in the file.

Comment 2. Procedures for drawing control should provide for listing all drawings and recording the revisions they have undergone, their present status, and the number of copies needed; distributing and receiving the drawings; filing of void drawings; and handling of shop, and as-built drawings. Recording of drawing revisions and drawing status may be accomplished by use of a drawing log at the project field office.

Item. A public utility, engaged in the construction of a major project, prepared drawings in its centralized engineering department. These drawings were then mailed to the site. However, no record was made of shipments mailed, nor did personnel on site check the items received. Consequently, several hundred drawings were lost in the mail, their absence was not detected in a timely fashion, and they had to be re-created on a crash basis.

5. Physical security, especially:

   (a) Access restrictions.

   (b) Reproduction requirements (i.e., backup copies).

Comment 3. If tight security for drawing copies is not necessary, the owner may distribute one reproducible copy of a drawing to the contractor, in lieu of numerous "hard" copies. This procedure is less costly than tight security measures and more convenient for both parties—the contractor being relieved of the need to make "contingency" copies. Reproducible copies should not be distributed, however, unless the owner is sure the contractor has sound procedures for retrieving superseded drawings.

6. Drawing changes, in respect to:
   (a) Extent of the research, evaluation, and justification required.
   (b) Criteria for the review and approval of the amended drawings after completion.

   Comment 4. Before a change is authorized, consideration should be given to the impact of the change on existing inventories of materials, or on construction already in place.

Physical Security over Drawings

Objective

Evaluate the job-site document control system.

Tasks

Examine the job-site document control system to determine whether all pertinent documents are distributed properly and in timely fashion, are appropriately filed, and can be readily retrieved.

Comment 1. It is desirable that field and home-office records be consolidated when the project is completed. To facilitate this, the job-site document control system (that contains the field records) should eventually become part of a master file maintained by the owner for all projects.

The examination should include:

A. Reviewing procedures for receipt and distribution of all job-site documents.

B.   Reviewing the file system to determine whether:

1.   It embodies the following (generally appropriate) file categories: contract documents and correspondence by contract number, incoming and outgoing letters, construction schedules, progress reports, the drawing file (taking care to retain superseded revisions and mark them void), insurance certificates, photographs, progress payments, back charges, change-orders and claims, contractor evaluations, permits and licenses, test results, and telephone and contact memoranda.

2.   It provides for keeping track of documents removed from files and promotes their timely return.

Comment 2.   The best system is useless if original documents are not tracked with a view toward securing their return to the files.

CHAPTER THIRTEEN

Claims and Change-Orders

Timely Evaluation and Optimal Resolution of Claims

Objective

Evaluate the operation of the claims-processing function.

> *Comment 1.* In this discussion a claim is assumed to be a request —appropriately supported by facts and circumstances—from a contractor for additional funds or a time extension. If the owner or his construction manager finds the claim to be justified and additional funds due, he or she writes a "change-order" to the original purchase order (or makes an amendment to the original contract). If the owner or his construction manager and the contractor cannot agree on a claim, either side could institute legal proceedings or apply for arbitration, if applicable.

Tasks

Review the claims department organization structure, staffing, policies and procedures to determine approvals by the appropriate parties and effectiveness in (1) minimizing exposure to claims that could otherwise be expected (on the basis of experience), and (2) processing claims that do occur promptly and at least cost.

> *Comment 2.* The best way to minimize exposure to claims is to identify potential claims early on, work toward optimum resolution, and eliminate their causes.

Expeditious settlements will be facilitated by recognition of *incipient* claims. One avenue to recognition is a periodic, preferably weekly, coordination meeting at which construction personnel, including outside contractors, bare actual or emerging problems. It is important for coordination meetings to operate within an orderly framework, including an agenda and minutes; the minutes offer a starting point for researching potential claims and for allaying damages.

The reasons given by contractors for claiming additional compensation include, but are not limited to:

Inconsistencies, errors, or omissions pertaining to the contract.

Errors on the part of the owner or his agents, including untimely or obstructive actions.

Unavailability of the site, right-of-way, or access.

Differing site conditions.

Forced deviations from the contemplated or planned work sequence.

Changes in the contemplated work schedule or forced deviations from it (whether delays or accelerations).

Changes in the nature of the work or additions to it.

Changes resulting from licensing or regulatory restrictions.

The review should involve:

A. Determining whether the organizational structure and policies and procedures of the claims department have been reviewed and approved by top management.

B. Interviewing persons who perform, review, and approve the completion of desired operational and internal accounting control procedures such as:

    1. Recurring reviews of documents to identify potential claims:

        (a) To ascertain the adequacy of the reviews in the light of:

            The documents covered (which should include (1) reports tracking the status of all change-orders and (2) coordination meeting minutes and conference reports).

            Their findings.

            Any recommendations for actions to minimize exposure.

(b)   To determine whether the documents have been reviewed and approved by appropriate management personnel.

2.   Tracking of potential and actual claims from initial identification to final disposition and evaluation of claims for estimated exposure:

(a)   To determine whether the tracking reports have been reviewed and approved by the appropriate supervisory or management personnel.

(b)   To verify the status of claims appearing on the report by reference to sources and to assess the reliability of the sources.

Item.   We reviewed a utility's claims management system. In the process we discovered an "inventory" of un-evaluated claims of more than $5 million. More significantly, we found that no system was in place for early (1) recognition of potential problems, (2) identification of capricious claims, and (3) settlement in timely, fair, and cost-effective fashion. We submitted a set of 15 recom-mendations to redress the conditions.

(c)   To compare the most recent tracking report to its predecessor and verify the propriety of any items carried from the earlier report.

Comment 3.   Numbering of claims helps to assure their being monitored into resolution or disposition. Stated differently, it makes "droppage" of previously reported claims difficult, and assures continuing attention to poten-tial problems.

(d)   To examine results of the recurring reviews, identifying new potential or asserted claims and determining whether all new claims have been accounted for on the tracking report.

(e)   To determine whether all claims have been classified preliminarily as to responsibility.

(f)   To attempt to assess the reasonableness of the estimated exposures.

(g) To attempt to assess the evaluation of exposure to claims in the same area at a later date or in different areas, both for reasonableness and for completeness (i.e., especially when there is information not previously known that might have a significant effect on the evaluations).

3. Testing the mathematical accuracy of reports.

4. Assessing the timeliness and effectiveness of actions taken to mitigate or defend against claims.

   Comment 4. The following techniques are among the more widely used for mitigating claims: second shifts instead of overtime, resequencing of the construction schedule or of operations, substitution of materials, and working in parallel rather than sequentially.

5. Assessing the role of the insurance manager with respect to claims management (i.e., as evidenced by reviewing the list of potential and actual claims and taking the necessary appropriate action).

6. Determining from legal counsel the number and nature of asserted claims and unasserted claims probable of assertion, and obtaining opinions about their outcome.

7. Evaluating the incidence of claims to determine whether the fault lies in systems weaknesses or in deficient application.

8. Determining whether:

   (a) The claims histories of particular contractors are filed for consideration in future bidding invitations and as input for assessing the owner's own engineering work as it relates to both design and construction.

   (b) The quality control or field engineering supervisors are doing everything they can to minimize claims.

Change-Orders Affecting Scope Limited to Instances of Necessity

Objective

Evaluate controls over change-orders.

Tasks

Review change-order policies and procedures and determine whether they have been approved by the appropriate parties and are complied with.

Comment 1. The higher the amount involved in a change-order, the higher the level of approval that should be required.

The review should include:

A. Determining whether the results of work performed to account for all proposed change-orders and to track their status have been reviewed and approved by appropriate supervisory and management personnel.

B. Determining whether proposed change-orders are researched and evaluated so that an in- or out-of-scope determination can be made. (Of course, in-scope work is performed for the contractor's account.)

C. Examining cost estimates for change-orders:

1. To determine whether the estimates have been reviewed and approved by appropriate supervisory personnel.

2. To determine, by examining evidence, and if necessary by questioning persons involved and observing procedures directly, whether (in the case of estimates prepared by a contractor) the estimates were verified by persons independent of the contractor and of others whose compensation may be affected by achievement of the estimates.

3. To check cost estimates against sources, assessing the reliability of the sources and of research for the estimates, if necessary by actively seeking information that may contradict conclusions.

D. Examining provisions for mandatory shopping (for price/quantity optimums) as a basis to negotiating change-orders:

1. To determine whether:

(a) The results of such shopping were reviewed by and approved by management.

(b) Those who performed the shopping were independent of (i.e., had no personal stake in) the change-order negotiations.

2. To evaluate the reliability of the sources on which the shopping findings are based, if necessary, by actively seeking information that may contradict these findings.

CHAPTER FOURTEEN

Materials

Vendor Cost, Quality, and Delivery Monitored

Objective

Evaluate the effectiveness of the procurement function.

Tasks

Review procurement policies and established procedures to determine whether they are complied with and whether operational and internal accounting controls are functioning as planned.

> *Comment 1.* The objectives of an effective procurement function are to ensure that materials are available when needed, have been obtained at optimum cost, and are of appropriate quality.
>
> The following steps were defined with the owner in mind. However, frequently some part of project procurement will be handled by contractors. In that case, it is appropriate for the owner to review the contractors' procurement functions. Most of the steps should apply to such reviews as well.

The review should involve:

A. Evaluating the functioning of operational and internal accounting controls, as discussed herein, on the basis of information obtained by questioning persons who perform the procedures and supervisors who approve that performance.

B. Investigating material-related costs, including carrying charges, and transportation costs, to determine whether:

1. Recommendations for procuring materials, including documentation of research and evaluation supporting the recommendations, have been reviewed and approved by appropriate management personnel.

2. Policies and established procedures covering the following points have been properly researched and evaluated:

    (a) Competitive buying requirements, including those for negotiated buying contracts and competitive bidding by suppliers.

    Comment 2. Close attention should be given to field procurement of bulk quantities of construction materials such as lumber, electrical connectors, formwork, temporary supports, and wire, which often tends to be performed in informal fashion.

    (b) Material requirements for the entire project, that is, what items are needed and when.

    Comment 3. It may be possible to combine material requirements for the construction project with other (operating) procurement requirements. The cost-effectiveness of this option should be considered. Sometimes construction material requirements may not be totally known, as, for example, when fast track is used. In such cases, reliance on estimates may be appropriate for negotiating purposes.

    Item. Buyers of construction materials may contract for purchases of "garden variety" items such as fractional horsepower motors, valves, bearings, etc. It is possible to compare the acquisition costs for these items with prices paid by operating storerooms. In one study construction purchasers paid more than 35 percent above the prices paid by operating storeroom buyers. Coordination can result not only in price standardization, but in additional quantity discounts. (And, separate purchasing agencies may also compete with each other, helping to drive up the cost of materials in scarce supply.)

     (c)   Lead times for ordering, especially of custom or specialty items.

     (d)   Determination of order quantities (and reorder points when appropriate) based on consideration of unit prices (adjusted for quantity discounts), ordering and carrying costs, administrative and vendor lead time, and inventory safety levels.

C.   Investigating the handling of purchase orders, as follows:

  1.   Authorization by:

     (a)   Determining whether purchase orders have been reviewed and approved.

     (b)   Comparing purchase orders to requisition and files for material and resolving inconsistencies.

  2.   Accounting by:

     (a)   Determining whether reports accounting for the status of open purchase orders have been reviewed and approved by supervisory personnel.

     (b)   Examining reports accounting for the status of sequentially numbered purchase orders to determine whether open purchase orders have been appropriately investigated and followed up to minimize the risk of nonavailability.

     (c)   Determining, by examining evidence and, if necessary, by questioning persons involved and observing procedures, whether procurement personnel have no connection with computer operations, receiving, and invoice approval.

     (d)   Reviewing open purchase orders to determine whether there are significant commitments to buy at prices in excess of market, and if so, assessing the impact of the commitments on the budget, with a view toward possible cancellation and "reshopping."

Site Materials Management

Objective

Evaluate policies and procedures governing materials management.

Tasks

Review policies and procedures relative to receiving, storing, and issuing of materials; test compliance; determine whether operational and internal accounting controls are functioning as planned. This review should cover the following:

A.   Procurement scheduling, by determining whether schedules:
1.   Exist for all major equipment and materials (designating any special parties responsible for procurement and indicating original site delivery date, current estimated delivery date, and date needed on site).
2.   Are reviewed regularly to assure that delivery dates support the current construction schedule and that adequate storage facilities are available on site.

B.   Expediting by assessing the adequacy of material delivery dates in relation to construction schedules.

Comment 1.   It is suggested that a material and equipment expediter be appointed to ensure deliveries when needed.

Item.   In scheduling delivery of structural items, planners were oblivious to vendors' prescribed delivery times. Subsequently, certain vendors added 15 percent of the material cost for "rush" delivery. This cost—together with similar costs—could have been averted by better planning and coordination of procurement activities with drawing preparation.

C.   Receiving and returning goods to and from vendors, specifically:
1.   Initial recording, as follows:
(a)   By observing receiving department procedures to assess the adequacy and effectiveness of counting, weighing, and inspection routines.

Item.   In theory, where materials are purchased F.O.B. factory, title to those goods resides in the owner from the moment of their delivery to the common carrier. Contrariwise, if goods are purchased F.O.B. site, they do not become the responsibility of the owner until they pass into his storeroom. Thus, F.O.B. points are important to determining who should file claims for in-transit damage. Further, the right to file a claim may expire after a two-year period. In one instance, claims valued at $400,000 were lost simply because responsibility for filing had not been determined as between the owner and the vendor.

(b)   By reviewing exception reports and questioning receiving department personnel about the incidence of discrepancies in the nature, quality, and quantity of goods received.

(c)   By determining, on the basis of inspection and exception reports, and, if necessary, by questioning personnel and observing procedures whether receiving department personnel are insulated from procurement, invoice approval, and accounting and computer operations functions. (Establishing independence of these activities from receiving fosters thorough incoming inspection).

Comment 2.   Certain finished materials cannot be tested without inflicting damage. For example, assume that precious metal bars are to be received. The purchase orders pertaining to those metals should have specified the tests to be applied, and the certifications to be affixed. (If the purchase orders did not, after-the-fact test requirements could be costly.) With respect to such items, quality certifications should be reviewed and controlled on the same basis as in-house inspection reports.

Under certain conditions (nuclear projects) it will be necessary to set up procedures to account for rejections to make certain that they are cleared and that materials become available for construction.

2.   Inputting and updating of goods-received records, as follows:

(a)   For completeness, by determining whether:

The architect or engineer has provided field construction teams with a bill of materials specifying what is to be bought and if so whether field supervisors have reviewed the bill together with construction drawings to detect omissions of materials or equipment.

All open documents have been accounted for in reports reviewed and approved by management.

Persons who either prepare or approve input and review reports have no connection with computer operations.

(b)   For accuracy, as follows:

By determining whether input edit reports have been reviewed and approved by appropriate supervisory personnel and whether errors and discrepancies in input (such as batch totals not matching, goods received with no corresponding purchase order, and invalid part numbers) were investigated and rectified.

By evaluating measures taken to follow up on returned goods.

D.   Transferring of material from stores into construction in progress, by determining:

1.   Whether the requisitions have been reviewed and approved by appropriate supervisory personnel.

2.   Whether there are any significant disparities between the requisitions and technical specifications (determined largely on the basis of documented comparisons and on-site inspections).

Comment 3. Significant numbers of requisitions for replacement of spoiled or pilfered material could indicate inadequate supervision at the construction site or inadequate site security.

3.   How the requisitions are accounted for, as follows:

(a)   By determining whether reports accounting for material requisitions have been reviewed and approved by appropriate supervisory personnel.

(b)   By evaluating measures (including programmed procedures) taken to follow up on missing requisitions.

4.   How the requisitions are input and updated, as follows:

(a)   In respect to accuracy, by determining whether:

Appropriate supervisory personnel have reviewed and approved the results of procedures to ensure that material requisition information is accurately input and updated.

All input and updated computer reports have been reviewed and all rejections of input items and discrepancies (for example, nonmatching batch totals) have been investigated and resolved.

(b) In respect to validity, as follows:

By evaluating the functioning of operational and internal accounting controls (based largely on information obtained by questioning persons who perform and approve the control procedures) and determining the nature of errors and the corrective actions taken.

By determining, by such means as examining batches of input documents (i.e., copies of the requisitions), whether controls over completeness and accuracy of output and update (designed to ensure that only valid and authorized transactions were processed) were reviewed and approved by appropriate supervisors.

E. Storage and record keeping:

1. By determining whether stockroom policies and procedures:

    (a) Have been reviewed and approved by appropriate supervisory or management personnel.

    (b) Provide for:

    Security, including restricted access.

    If appropriate, cycle count procedures, covering:

    Methods of verification (i.e., counting or weighing).

    The nature and level of second counts.

    Supervision.

    Custodial controls associated with inventories (i.e., check counts applied where persons performing original cycle counts also have custody of inventories or maintain accounting records).

    Timing of cycle counts (i.e., after receiving and issuance activity has ceased for the day). Normally, cycle counts would apply to items used repetitively; generally, to reduce effort it would be advantageous to count items at or near the reorder point.

Accuracy of counting.

Extent of cycle counts (held to a minimum by computer selection of items to be counted).

Resolution of discrepancies between book and physical counts.

2. By inspecting inventory storage facilities, to evaluate:

(a) Systems and procedures, including:

Measures for preventing unauthorized access.

Methods for locating stored materials (i.e., identification systems or inventory logs that indicate locations of various items and also record special maintenance needs).

(b) The materials themselves, for:

Arrangement, that is, optimum accessibility.

> *Comment 4.* Aside from the likelihood that materials will be stored in the wrong area or that incorrect materials will be issued into construction-in-progress, a poorly laid out stockroom invites excessive storage and handling costs.

Availability of materials handling equipment.

> *Comment 5.* Distribution of materials within a project is as important as receipt of materials from the outside. If crane capacity is insufficient, traffic flows will need to be diverted around heavy items, or items will be subject to costly disassembly.

Preplanning.

> *Comment 6.* Unless reasonable estimates are made in advance of space requirements, both in terms of weight to be stored and cubic dimensions, rehandling of the materials may be necessary.

Physical protection.

> *Comment 7.* To the extent that articles are sensitive to heat, humidity, or air pollution, special protective arrangements need to be made to avoid costly rework and cleanup.

The existence of apparent overstocking or stocking of obsolete items.

Comment 8. Excessive or obsolete inventories could indicate poor buying practices and inadequate research and evaluation of drawing changes and value analysis proposals.

3. If appropriate, by testing cycle count procedures, as follows:

    (a) Determining whether cycle count results have been reviewed and approved by appropriate supervisory personnel.

    Comment 9. In general, differences between physical and book counts reflect on the effectiveness of control (physical as well as record keeping) over the receipt or issuance of materials, maintenance of data, or input of materials transactions. If differences are numerous, it is important not only to evaluate measures taken to resolve them, but to look into the causes of the discrepancies.

    (b) Examining the pattern of adjustments to either the records or the physical count, and, if necessary, questioning personnel and observing procedures directly, to evaluate the adequacy of custodial controls relative to cycle counts and the effectiveness of counting procedures.

    (c) Performing test counts, using, if appropriate, computerized techniques to select items for counting.

F. Management of surplus materials, by reviewing procedures for disposal, either by sale or by transfer to other jobs, to determine whether they are carried out expeditiously, and, when disposal is by sale, whether fair value is received and the amount credited to the project.

CHAPTER FIFTEEN

Labor

Union Contracts Observed

Objective

Evaluate compliance with labor contracts.

Tasks

Review specific policies and established procedures associated with union labor to determine whether they are in accord with contract provisions and are complied with. The review should include:

A. Determining, by examining evidence and, if necessary, by questioning personnel and observing procedures directly, whether:
   1. Break, rest, and other allowances incorporated in labor rates are being enforced scrupulously.
   2. Grievances by both management and employees are processed in accordance with contract terms.
B. When appropriate, determining whether committees (or "courts") convened to place blame for poor workmanship are functioning in accordance with union contract terms.
C. Investigating employee turnover to see whether it exceeds reasonable limits and, if so, whether corrective action is being taken.
D. Determining, through direct observation and by inspection of records, whether appropriate employee training and qualification testing are maintained.

E. Determining whether "learning curves" are appropriately considered in evaluations of employee activity.

F. When appropriate, determining whether wage rates and policies governing cost-of-living adjustments, productivity standards, and incentives comply with applicable union contracts, area labor conditions, or both.

G. Examining union contract renewal dates.

Comment. If there is any likelihood of a strike on the expiration of a contract, consideration should be given to rearranging construction activities to minimize the impact. In addition, contingency planning might be advisable to provide for increased project cost and duration.

H. Determining whether project labor is employed under a project agreement and, if so, reviewing the agreement for compliance with all terms and conditions.

Labor Productivity Measured

Objective

Evaluate the effectiveness with which labor productivity is monitored.

Comment 1. Monitoring of labor productivity is important not only with cost-plus, unit-price, or time-and-material contracts, but also lump-sum contracts. Heavy idleness will almost certainly impact costs. To the extent idleness is unavoidable, it should be considered in estimating costs for the operation on future projects. To the extent idleness is due to poor supervision or excessive crewing, the contractor may be responsible, although indemnification would be difficult to obtain. Productivity measurement is especially important where some personnel of a contractor work on a lump-sum basis and others on separately negotiated engineering changes, not necessarily lump-sum. (With dual contractual arrangements of this sort, the measurement process may be complicated by the difficulty of identifying workers subject to one arrangement or the other; in such situations special worker badges or other identification may be necessary.)

Tasks

Review policies and procedures for monitoring labor productivity to determine whether they have been approved by the appropriate parties, cover all significant aspects, and are complied with. The review should involve:

A. Determining whether policies and procedures for monitoring labor productivity:

1. Have been reviewed and approved by management.

Comment 2. On large, complex projects, especially where some of the work is performed by personnel working for the owner or the construction manager, labor productivity measurement techniques such as work/no work observations may be used.

Item. Observation of construction workers on a Texas nuclear project showed that the men were working during less than one-third of the observations. However, in many instances idleness was caused by lack of supervision, lack of instructions, lack of materials, and lack of tools. It was determined that effective coordination of construction operations could double the work observations, resulting in a lessened need for new workers on this cost-plus project.

Comment 3. Some productivity approximations can be applied to professional personnel. For example, design engineers should account for their time; catch-all time accounts should be avoided; time charges should be subject to approval; time charges should be evaluated against budgets; and, productivity measures—such as numbers of drawings produced—should be used wherever practical to determine how time has been spent. (Judicious timekeeping becomes particularly important where work is performed by the same people for more than one project or more than one owner.)

2. Provide for:

(a) Documentation of attendance reviews.

(b) Documentation of observations of idle time.

    (c)   Reviews to ascertain whether work is conducted productively.

    (d)   Procedures for corrective action relative to no-work situations, monitoring contractor supervision, and counteracting contractor supervisory weaknesses.

B.   Examining the minutes of the superintendent's or the general foreman's meetings for discussion of labor productivity and improvement measures.

C.   Evaluating the functioning of operational and internal accounting controls, as discussed herein, with reliance on information obtained by questioning persons who perform the procedures and supervisors who approve that performance.

D.   Determining whether reports summarizing the results of monitoring labor productivity:

    1.   Have been reviewed and approved by management.

    2.   Include significant findings, recommendations for action, and information on the status of previously recommended actions.

E.   Determining whether appropriate supervisory personnel have reviewed and approved reports on:

    1.   Attendance.

    2.   Idle time.

    3.   Worker efficiency.

    4.   Contractor supervision.

F.   Evaluating labor productivity reports as follows:

    1.   For the completeness and accuracy of the data on which they are based—on the basis of information obtained from field observations and questioning of field supervisors (and if possible workers as well) at the work sites.

    2.   For the reasonableness and propriety of findings (including recommendations for action)—on the basis of information obtained by reviewing documentation and conducting independent field observations and inquiries.

    Comment 4. Field observations, especially of individual workers, must be carried out with discretion because of possible difficulties with unions.

Affirmative Action Compliance

Objective

Evaluate the reporting of compliance with affirmative action goals.

Tasks

Review affirmative action reports to determine whether they have been reviewed and approved by appropriate parties and evaluate coverage. The review should involve:

A. Evaluating the functioning of operational and internal accounting controls, as discussed herein, with reliance on information obtained by questioning persons who perform the procedures and supervisors who approve that performance.

   Comment.   Relative to malfunctioning of operational and internal accounting controls, it is possible to conduct searches for untoward events which would have been or should have been prevented by proper functioning of controls. If a shortfall occurs in the hire of a minority, a determination should be made whether the original commitment was realistic; and, if so, whether the breakdown occurred in locating *sources* of minorities, in training, or in certification. Once the deficiency has been identified, controls may need to be strengthened correspondingly.

B. Determining whether periodic affirmative action progress reports:
   1. Are reviewed and approved by management.
   2. Provide the following:
      (a) Explanations of failure to accomplish goals and recommendations for corrective action.
      (b) Assignments of responsibility for followup on recommendations.
      (c) If appropriate, information on the status of followup on prior recommendations.
   3. Use the same units of measurement as the definition of goals.
C. Reviewing (on a sampling basis) data used in reports for accuracy and completeness.

CHAPTER SIXTEEN

Accounting and Reporting

Integrity of Computer Operations Maintained

Objective

Evaluate the functioning of computer operations with emphasis on accuracy and completeness controls.

Tasks

Review computer operations to determine whether controls are functioning as planned. The review should involve evaluating:

A.   The functioning of operational and internal accounting controls, as discussed herein (with reliance on information supplied by persons who perform and approve the procedures).

B.   Controls over program and data security, as follows:

1.   By determining—on the basis of such evidence as signatures of approval, documentation of the nature and extent of review procedures performed, and logs or memoranda relating to questions, exceptions, and rejections—whether appropriate MIS supervisory personnel have reviewed and approved compliance with operator instructions (i.e., in regard to use of systems software, job set-up, restart, and recovery procedures) with a view to assuring that no unauthorized changes are made to program and data files in the course of:

(a)   Loading the files into the computer, running them, and unloading them from the computer.

(b)   Storing the files and transporting them between the computer and the storage area.

2.   By determining whether the systems analyst or any programmers have access to any program or data files (i.e., by reviewing the security of the file library, observing computer operations, examining file and computer usage logs, and questioning of personnel).

C.   Security over the computer and its peripherals, in respect to:

1.   Emergency plans, as follows:

(a)   By obtaining an understanding of the nature of the emergency plans from a study of written procedures and direct questioning of key EDP personnel (noting disparities between respondents' conceptions of their roles and the written procedures).

(b)   By observing the location and condition of features essential to carrying out the plans, such as protective coverings, telephones, and power-off switches.

(c)   By inquiring into the nature and results of emergency plan tests and reviewing related reports, memoranda, and other documentation.

2.   Fire prevention and detection, as follows:

(a)   By determining, through observation and inquiry, whether:

The computer center is subject to external or internal fire hazards.

There are fire-detection and firefighting devices (and if there are, noting their location).

(b)   By reviewing:

Reports covering reviews made before the computer systems were installed and reviews made by insurance or fire department personnel of electrical systems and fire-detection and firefighting devices, noting factors considered and decisions reached.

Written procedures covering the testing of fire-related systems and equipment.

Reports, certificates, memoranda, tags, and other documents regarding results of the tests conducted.

3. Water damage prevention and detection, as follows:

   (a) By determining through observation and inquiry (including checks on the availability of insurance coverage) whether the computer is vulnerable to flood, hurricane, or water main burst.

   (b) By determining through observation and by querying EDP or maintenance personnel, whether the structural surroundings of the computer center provide for protection against water pipe bursts, flooding on higher floors, and other internal water-related threats.

4. Prevention and detection of damage from air conditioning failure, as follows:

   (a) By reviewing reports and memoranda regarding the power and air conditioning systems, noting the factors considered and the decisions reached; also reviewing any pertinent recommendations made by the power company.

   (b) By determining through observation, inquiry, and review of reports, memoranda, temperature/humidity charts, and any other pertinent data, whether the power and air conditioning systems are being adequately monitored and whether, if any unfavorable conditions exist, necessary corrective action is being taken.

5. Protection against less well-known environmental threats, as follows:

   (a) By determining through observation, inquiry, and review of reports and memoranda whether the computer center is vulnerable to any of the following:

   Disasters, including earthquakes, windstorms, and explosions.

   Emanations, including those of a gaseous, microwave, magnetic, or radioactive nature.

   Airborne particles such as dust, sand, or the solid matter in smoke.

(b)   By reviewing reports and memoranda to determine what action, if any, has been taken.

6.   Protection against hostile acts, including both intrusion and physical attack, as follows:

(a)   By evaluating, on the basis of an examination of written procedures, information from personnel, and direct observation of activities, security against hostile acts, noting particularly the extent to which unauthorized individuals are restricted in access to the computer center.

(b)   By examining control lists for keys, badges, and other access devices and ascertaining whether all listed individuals do, in fact, require access to the computer center.

(c)   By reviewing reports and memoranda regarding the exposure to physical attack or intrusion, noting factors considered and conclusions reached.

(d)   By determining whether physical security procedures are effective after normal working hours and on weekends.

(e)   By evaluating practices (relying chiefly on information supplied by supervisors) regarding preemployment security checks, rotation of duties, issuance of access devices, and termination procedures and by comparing the practices to authorized policies and procedures.

(f)   By determining rotation policies as indicated in organization charts, employee lists, and vacation schedules, and assessing the adequacy of the policies and the extent to which they are adhered to.

7.   Back-up provisions, as follows:

(a)   By evaluating, on the basis of written procedures and other descriptive matter, the scope of the security back-up system, in terms of hardware, software, documentation, files, personnel, and related aspects.

(b)   By questioning persons associated with the back-up system as to their understanding of the system and the associated procedures, noting disparities between their conceptions and the approved procedural ones.

(c)   By evaluating the operation of back-up facilities, on the basis of reports, memoranda, and contracts.

(d) By determining, through review of file directory control records, as well as inspection of back-up files, whether the files are sufficiently comprehensive to allow for reconstruction of current transactions.

(e) By evaluating procedures for updating back-up programs and documentation. (This could be done by seeing to what extent recent modifications to primary programs have been reflected in the back-up programs and in the documentation at the back-up location.)

(f) Determining, on the basis of reports, memoranda, and other data, whether the back-up system has been recently tested and, if so, whether deficiencies have been corrected.

(g) By evaluating, through physical inspection, the security of the storage and transportation facilities associated with the back-up system.

D. The efficiency and effectiveness of MIS operations in the following areas:

1. Data conversion, as follows:

(a) By determining through examining documents and control logs and, if appropriate, questioning data conversion personnel, whether user department personnel are adhering to written instructions regarding data input and conversion.

Item. A client's hardware configuration experienced input-capability limitations. This resulted in processing delays and operator overtime. We recommended an upgrading of main frame computer hardware, to avoid overtime and to speed service.

(b) By evaluating, through examination of conversion department systems documentation and querying of data conversion personnel, the documentation of scheduling, data sequence, data format, and verification procedures.

(c) By determining, through direct observation of conversion personnel in action, examination of punched cards and control logs, and information obtained by querying computer operations personnel, whether these personnel are adhering to written instructions.

(d)   By determining whether a work schedule is in effect that shows the flow of work into, through, and out of the data conversion section and, if so, evaluating the schedule for accuracy and completeness.

(e)   By determining, through inquiry, observation, and review of logs, reports, or memoranda, whether there are bottlenecks in the conversion area and whether schedules and deadlines are being met.

(f)   By assessing the performance of the productivity reporting and control system as follows:

Examining standards, production statistics, comparative reports and memoranda to ascertain whether all aspects of the system are in operation.

For selected operators and periods, tracing production statistics to supporting documentation, reperforming comparisons of actual productivity to standards, noting any apparent trends and investigating any sharp disparities or unusual indications.

(g)   By determining, through inquiry, observation of procedures, and review of source documents, whether standard-size batches are established, source documents are properly designed, operators are properly supervised and remain at their work stations during normal work periods, and work assignments are efficiently distributed.

(h)   By determining, through inquiry and review of input documents and data file record layouts, whether any of the following conditions exist: data fields no longer needed are being converted, the same data is being converted more than once, or constant data (such as a date) is being converted separately for each transaction.

(i)   By determining, through appropriate systems documentation and questioning of user department, systems and programming personnel, whether program controls have been substituted for key verification whenever practicable (i.e., where key verification is used, it is applied only to critical fields).

(j)   By evaluating the size of the data conversion staff in relation to the work flow, as follows:

Reviewing schedules, control logs, and other records to
assess the regularity with which work arrives, and time,
production, and other reports to determine the extent of
idle time.

Determining whether work is contracted out or whether
such a practice has been considered.

Comment 2. There are various methods of converting
data, including direct input via CRTs by user departments,
keypunch by MIS personnel, and submission of MIS
through the optical character reader (OCR) of input forms
prepared by user departments. Therefore, not all of the
above data conversion tests may be applicable.

2.   Processing of data, as follows:

(a)   By reviewing machine room operating procedures and,
through direct observation, determining whether the
procedures are followed.

(b)   By reviewing run manuals, and for selected programs determining whether they include:

A brief description of the program and its purpose.

A flow chart showing the sequence and relationship of
programs and files.

Special set-up and take-down instructions.

A list of messages and programmed halts and action to be
taken on each halt.

(c)   By evaluating, on the basis of information obtained by
questioning personnel and by direct observation of ma-
chine-room procedures, the physical layout of the machine
room from the point of view of operating efficiency.

(d)   By evaluating the scheduling process in accordance with
the type of system used, as follows:

For systems not utilizing multiprogramming, determining
whether the scheduling was accomplished with the aid of a
formal technique, such as a Gantt chart.

For multiprogramming systems, determining whether program characteristics are considered in the scheduling process.

(e) Evaluating scheduling efficiency, as follows:

Determining, by inquiry and direct observation, whether files, programs, and operators are in the right place at the right time.

Determining, on the basis of memoranda and other records, that time, activity, and utilization reports have been reviewed by appropriate MIS personnel and recommendations for corrective action implemented.

For selected time periods, reviewing time, activity, and utilization reports, and investigating:

Any marked deviations from established patterns evident in current operations.

All delays, determining what, if any, corrective measures have been taken (i.e., repair of equipment, rescheduling of tasks, or removal of inefficient operators).

Operating procedures, run manuals, and schedules for any indications of weakness.

Determining whether any analyses have been performed with respect to potential benefits of changing shifts, expanding or reducing overtime, or using service bureaus, and:

If so, evaluating the analyses on the basis of the related written findings (as embodied in memoranda or reports).

If not, deciding whether an analysis would be appropriate, in consultation with data processing supervisors and with consideration of such factors as the cost of in-house salaries and of service bureaus.

Evaluating the monitoring of computer utilization (using information from pertinent memoranda and reports) for comprehensiveness and for the efficiency with which problems identified are remedied.

3. File storage and protection, as follows:

By reviewing written procedures covering file protection devices and techniques, inspecting the files and file cases, and questioning the persons who handle the files—determining whether there are file protection rings, external and internal labels, and protected boundaries.

By reviewing processing logs and rerun reports—determining whether any reruns are caused by the absence of protective devices and techniques.

By examining data file library records and systems and program documentation—determining whether record-retention requirements are adhered to.

By querying appropriate parties directly and reviewing memoranda and reports—determining:

Whether there is a periodic review and purging of obsolete or duplicate data records or files.

Whether there is a periodic review of file storage and organization.

By reviewing selected record layouts for repetitive characters, blanks and other indications—determining whether data compression techniques might be useful.

By reviewing applicable procedures and examining logs, labels, and other indications—determining whether prescribed policies are followed for cleaning and testing tapes and disks.

By reviewing processing logs or rerun reports for evidence of tape errors and examining records of cleaning or testing or external tape labels—determining whether tapes having errors were cleaned and tested according to the prescribed schedule.

Cost Accumulation: Timely, Accurate, and Complete

Objective

Evaluate policies and procedures for controlling cost accumulation.

Tasks

Review cost-accumulation policies and procedures to determine whether they have been approved by the appropriate parties, cover all significant controls, and are complied with.

> *Comment 1.* The cost-accumulation system should accumulate information for use in monitoring actual performance against budget and other cost-performance indicators.
>
> This section assumes that the owner runs the cost system. However, in many operations this responsibility devolves on the construction manager or general contractor. Where this is the case, the steps that follow should be modified accordingly.

The review should involve examining:

A. Cost-accumulation policies and procedures, to determine whether they:
1. Have been reviewed and approved by management.
2. Provide for:
   (a) Review and registration of invoices on receipt, subject to subsequent adjustment.
   (b) Accounting for all transactions affecting construction costs, including goods and services received for which invoices have not yet been furnished.
   (c) A method of ensuring that only valid and authorized accounts payable transactions are accurately input and updated.
   (d) Procedures to review and approve payments.

B. The functioning of operational and internal accounting controls as discussed herein, with reliance on information obtained by questioning persons who perform the procedures and supervisors who approve such performance.

> *Comment 2.* The investigation of cost accumulation should involve analysis of contracts on a sample basis. The selection should consist of representative construction and consultant contracts.

C. The checking of significant invoices, as follows:

1. By determining whether the results of the checking of invoices have been reviewed and approved, prior to being entered into accounts payable, by the following:

(a) The project manager (construction manager, general contractor, architect, or engineer), for validity of the contractor and subcontractor percentage of completion, quality, propriety of account codings, and other technical considerations.

Comment 3. The account codings of these invoices should be detailed enough to mirror actual construction activities.

(b) The financial officer, for compliance of invoices with contract and payment terms and for accuracy of clerical computations, including retention and total prior payments.

2. By determining, on the basis of evidence and if necessary by questioning personnel and observing procedures directly, whether invoices are checked and approved by persons functionally independent of procurement, receiving, and computer operations.

3. By evaluating the effectiveness with which clerical functions in connection with invoices (e.g., matching and checking of extensions and additions) are performed, if appropriate, through selective reperformance of these functions.

Comment 4. If any functions are performed by the computer, they can be rerun on a sample basis or by using a specially prepared computer program.

4. By determining whether adjustments to suppliers' accounts are documented and approved by appropriate supervisory personnel and evaluating adjustments for propriety and reasonableness.

D. The completeness of all construction reported as in progress, as follows:

1. By determining whether the results of procedures for accounting for all invoices have been reviewed and approved by appropriate supervisory personnel.

2. By determining, on the basis of evidence and if necessary by questioning personnel and observing procedures directly, whether persons who perform or review and approve procedures for accounting for all invoices have no connection with accounts payable control or with computer operations.

3. By examining reports that:

   (a) Identify invoices, as follows:

      Those received but not posted to accounts payable, ascertaining by direct observation the method of identification used (i.e., sequential numbering of invoices or entry into a control log).

      Those that should have been received but have not been (i.e., identified by computer matching of invoices received against the file of unmatched receiving reports).

   (b) Investigate the current status of the missing items, comparing the results to whatever investigation has already been carried out and resolving discrepancies.

      Comment 5. The purpose of the tests is to ensure that all cost-accumulation has been recorded. If cost-accumulation information is not complete, there may be an understatement of costs when actual costs are compared to physical completion. (These tests may be reduced in number and in scope if results indicate that controls are adequate.)

4. By examining cost-accumulation activity for the period under review, as follows:

   (a) To determine whether:

      All recurring entries were completely and accurately posted to the cost-accumulation records.

      All significant nonstandard journal entries were accurately posted to the cost-accumulation records.

      Any significant entries were not accounted for in the two previous steps.

   (b) To evaluate the reasonableness and propriety of entries (on the basis of explanations and supporting documents).

5. By performing a search for unrecorded liabilities, as follows:

> (a) Reviewing payments made subsequent to the end of the period, examining supporting documentation (especially invoices, receiving reports, and purchase orders), and determining whether liabilities were recorded in the proper period.
>
> (b) Examining unmatched invoices and receiving reports to determine whether they have been recorded as liabilities in the proper period.

E. The accuracy of input and update, as follows:

1. By determining whether the results of procedures designed to ensure that accounts payable invoices are accurately input have been reviewed and approved by appropriate supervisory personnel.

2. By determining, on the basis of evidence and, if necessary, by questioning personnel and observing procedures directly, whether persons performing or approving procedures to ensure accurate input and update of accounts payable transactions have no connection with maintaining an accounts payable control account or with computer operations.

3. By determining whether all applicable reports have had appropriate accuracy checks performed (such as manual agreement checks of batch totals after processing and review of exception and rejection reports) and that all discrepancies have been investigated and resolved by:

   (a) Selecting items to be checked, such as batch totals and items appearing on the reports.

   (b) Reperforming agreement checks of batch totals or investigating items appearing on the reports.

   (c) Comparing the results of this check with any existing documented investigation and resolving discrepancies.

4. If appropriate, by testing the accuracy of invoice batching by examining batch tapes and input documents and by recalculating batch totals.

F. Authorization controls, by determining whether:

1. Appropriate supervisory personnel have reviewed and approved

all input data (i.e., on an individual or batch basis) either after the establishment of controls over completeness and accuracy of input and update or immediately after processing.

2. Conditions exist that could allow an unauthorized transaction to be processed without timely discovery.

G. Subsidiary ledger tests, as follows:

1. By determining whether subsidiary ledgers (construction in progress, accounts payable, retention payable, and material stores) have been reconciled to the applicable general ledger accounts and whether those reconciliations have been reviewed and approved by appropriate supervisory or management personnel.

2. By determining, on the basis of evidence and if necessary by questioning personnel and observing procedures directly, whether persons associated with computer operations or with the functions of maintaining control accounts for the applicable reconciliation, or—in the case of stores—with maintaining custody of stores inventories, have been dissociated from reconciliation activities.

H. The physical state of construction in progress, as follows:

1. By evaluating the reasonableness of the recorded percentage of completion on the basis of the comparison between physical progress of construction and percentage-of-completion records.

2. By reviewing the work performed for *obvious* qualitative defects and comparing findings to the conclusions of reports on quality assurance and quality control as well as on routine in-line inspection reports.

3. By touring the construction site and determining whether any equipment is obsolete or idle and if so whether the owner is being charged for such equipment (or worse, whether he is being charged by more than one contractor).

4. By evaluating the propriety of amounts to be paid, as follows:

(a) Determining whether check signers have reviewed supporting documents before signing (on the basis of signatures on check packages, memos explaining refusal to approve, and other documentary evidence).

(b) Examining invoices to determine whether they have been

properly checked and approved prior to payment, and checking total-to-total agreement of invoices paid.

5. By determining whether invoices are effectively cancelled by, or under the control of, the signatories on a timely basis to prevent subsequent resubmission (in the process, examining check packages, questioning persons involved, and observing the procedures directly).

6. By examining payment policies to determine whether full advantage is taken of cash discounts (reviewing, in the process, invoice due dates, discounts, and owner cash-flow requirements) or, if no discounts are available, whether payments are being held until due dates.

I. Coding and summarization of cost-accumulation activity, as follows:

1. By determining whether:

   (a) The checking of input in connection with the coding of cost-accumulation activity to the cost-accumulation system has been reviewed and approved by appropriate supervisory personnel.

   (b) All input edits for coding of invoices have been adequately checked (by comparing invoices to input edits on a test basis).

   Comment 6. Codings are approved during detailed checking of invoices to ensure they are proper; the above two steps are designed to facilitate assessment of the accuracy with which approved codings are input and updated to the cost-accumulation system.

   (c) Summaries of cost-accumulation activity have been reviewed and approved by appropriate supervisory personnel.

2. By evaluating basic summarization control, through any or all of the following procedures:

   (a) Examining manual reconciliation of totals, testing clerical accuracy, and checking agreement with sources.

   (b) Investigating any discrepancies and comparing the results to those of the existing method of resolution.

(c)   Determining whether output from the cost-accumulation system accommodates all requirements of the owner's general ledger, as well as those of a legal and regulatory nature and those concerned with the tax credit and the energy credit.

J.   Controls over storage, issuance, and usage of checks, by seeing that physical security is maintained, that numbers are printed on or assigned to checks, and that usage is accounted for, preferably by persons independent of the custodian of unused checks.

K.   Controls over timekeeping, especially where the owner, or construction manager, employ their own forces on force-account work, by determining whether:

1.   Timekeeping procedures cover the entire force.

2.   The timekeepers are not affiliated in any way with the crafts they are monitoring.

3.   The time cards agree with the timekeepers' reports.

4.   The time spent is reconciled to a record of tasks accomplished to provide some indication of productivity.

L.   Contract retention release procedures, as follows:

1.   By determining whether:

(a)   The terms of the contract (purchase order) have been satisfied to the extent required by the specifications, drawings, and all other contract documents.

(b)   The retention release is partial or full.

(c)   All quality control requirements have been met.

2.   By reviewing the approvals required for retention release.

Exception Reporting

Objective

Evaluate status reports and the effectiveness with which they are utilized.

Tasks

Review the various project status reports to determine whether they accurately depict current status of project activities. Review the distribution of the reports to management and consider the timing, nature, and extent of corrective actions.

Comment. The three reports most likely to be in use in medium or large projects are the project progress report (usually prepared by the construction manager and issued monthly), the contractor's progress report (also generally monthly), and the contract status and cost reports, generally prepared monthly by the owner's accounting personnel.

The reviews should involve:

A. For project progress reports, determining whether:

  1. The reports address the following points: manpower and man-hours, actual versus scheduled progress (with photographs), actual versus forecast expenditures, construction problems, changes in schedule or scope of work, commencement and completion of preselected benchmark activities, and bulk quantity or man-hour unit rates (in cost-plus contracts).

  2. The following parties have contributed: the architect or engineer, and the managers for construction, contracts, licensing, cost and scheduling, and start-up.

  3. The reports contain a summary of significant activities that occurred during the period covered and identify current or potential problems and the remedial actions being taken.

B. For contractors' progress reports, determining whether the reports cover at least the following: actual versus scheduled progress, percentage completed, quantities of materials used, and man-hours expended.

C. For contract status and cost reports, determining whether the reports contain a description of the work and specify the contract or purchase order number, the type of contract (lump-sum, unit-price or cost-plus), the name of the contractor, the original and the current dollar commitment, the amount of payments to date, the percentage completed, the anticipated completion date, and remarks.

D. For all project status reports, determining whether the reports are distributed in a timely fashion to all management personnel who are concerned with the project.

Contractor Cost, Quality, and Delivery Performance Tracked

Objective

Evaluate the evaluation of contractor performance.

Tasks

Review established procedures for evaluating contractor performance, evaluate the coverage and determine whether the procedures have been approved by the appropriate parties. This review and evaluation should involve:

A.   Determining whether:

1.   Procedures governing contractor evaluation call for:

(a)   A specific recommendation for or against using the contractor for future work.

(b)   A comparison between dollars and man-hours originally estimated and dollars and man-hours ultimately contracted for.

(c)   A brief written description of the scope and nature of the work.

(d)   The handling of change-orders.

(e)   Assignment of unit cost for every significant work item in the contract including quantities and man-hour relationships.

(f)   An evaluation of the effectiveness of:

The home office group in supporting the field group.

The field group in providing proper supervision, safe working practices, and cooperation with other contractors, and in meeting construction equipment supply requirements.

(g)   A qualitative evaluation of work performed.

(h)   Comments on any aspect of performance, including additional work activities and overtime.

(i)   Comparing and collating the various monitoring reports to arrive at an ultimate or consensual evaluation.

Comment. This step assumes (1) that the results of tests monitoring contractor performance indicate that operational and internal accounting controls are functioning effectively, and (2) that other tests verify the completeness, accuracy, and validity of the supporting documentation.

2. The performance—cost, quality, and delivery—evaluations of contractors who have worked for the owner in recent years are stored in a central file for use in selecting contractors in the future, and that these evaluations are forwarded to responsible parties whenever they request information on a possible bidder.

Unfavorable Variances Monitored

Objective

Evaluate the monitoring of contractor performance.

Tasks

Review established procedures for monitoring compliance of contractors with contract provisions, and for following up on variations in cost, timeliness, and quality. Determine whether the procedures are being complied with, and evaluate them.

Comment 1. Where applicable, monitoring procedures should cover the construction manager; his performance may be more critical to the success of the project than that of contractors.

The review and evaluation should involve:

A. Evaluating the functioning of operational and internal accounting controls, as discussed herein, with heavy reliance on information obtained by questioning persons who perform and approve the applications of control procedures.

B. Determining whether the results of monitoring contractor compliance with contract provisions have been reviewed and approved by appropriate supervisory and management personnel.

C. Evaluating the review, using the documents prepared in connection with it as well as construction contracts or approved abstracts and, as appropriate, assessing the reliability of the sources cited in the documents.

D. Searching for any other information which may contradict the documented information.

E. Determining whether reports monitoring contractor performance in terms of cost, timeliness, and quality have been reviewed and approved by project management (on the basis of documentation of review procedures, questions and findings, and action taken).

Comment 2. The owner should look for a consensus in favor of the reports, their conclusions, and any corrective action to be taken, rather than for unanimous approval, which is frequently difficult to secure, especially relative to corrective action.

F. Evaluating the handling of variances, identified in monitoring contractor performance, as follows:

Comment 3. An audit or investigative trail should exist for variances. Essentially, there should be indications of the manner in which the problem was investigated (i.e., by telephone, mail, or site visit), of the persons who were contacted, and of the outcome of the investigation.

For variances existing in past but not present performance, corrective action may involve revisions to the system, steps to recover excessive costs, and inputs to guide future plans. If the variances are ongoing or can be predicted with reasonable certainty, corrective action may involve strengthening of crewing, substitutions of vendors, changes in materials, warnings, or dockings. The various options for corrective action should be discussed, the price tags for pursuing each estimated, and other pros or cons spelled out. The recommended measures should be based upon documented data.

If the variance affects scheduling, consideration may be given to a variety of techniques designed to bring construction back on schedule, for example, establishing second shifts or overtime, resequencing the schedule, working in parallel rather than sequentially, postponing overall target dates, and reducing test periods. Each technique is based on particular assumptions and none should be selected without full consideration of possible alternatives.

1. By determining whether the variances are investigated and acted on in timely fashion.

2. By assessing the appropriateness and reasonableness of action
taken on variations, in respect to:

(a) Cost, that is, cost reduction, by:

Substitution of materials.

> *Comment 4.* The concept of material substitution
> refers not merely to the substitution of one type of ma-
> terial over another but also to adaptation of materials on
> hand to different purposes than intended. In either case,
> substitution should be undertaken only after a careful
> weighing of the effects on the planned structure.

Use of prefabricated materials, for example, prefabricated
siding or flooring instead of poured concrete or standard
sheet metal construction.

Preassembly of materials, either off-site or at a separate
on-site preassembly area.

> *Comment 5.* The technique of preassembly is par-
> ticularly useful in work areas of limited space. When
> applied to structural steel, sheet metal, pipe supports,
> piping sections, reinforcing steel, and other structural
> constituents, preassembly usually results in cost and
> time savings.

Second shifts.

> *Comment 6.* Second shifts usually involve a premium
> in the range of 10 to 20 percent over single-shift opera-
> tions. This is much less than the additional costs of
> overtime. On the other hand, shift work suffers from two
> handicaps: the resistance of labor, especially unionized
> labor, and the difficulties of maintaining good
> supervision.

Overtime.

> *Comment 7.* In general, overtime should be performed
> only when preplanned and authorized. It requires notice
> to workers, supervision, and proper working conditions,
> that is, lighting, especially if out-of-doors. Studies have
> shown that too much overtime results in lessening of

productivity, sometimes below what could have been achieved had only a regular shift been worked. In evaluating the desirability of overtime, consideration should be given to worker productivity on second shifts.

Back charges to contractors.

Comment 8. Back charges represent reimbursement, by the party whose negligence or nonfulfillment of contractual obligations created excess costs. The reimbursed party may be another contractor or the owner (for example, if the owner's construction manager undertook the needed work). Adequate documentation is a prerequisite for imposing back charges.

(b)   Timeliness, that is, improvement of time utilization by:

Resequencing operations.

Comment 9. Resequencing is subject to constraints imposed by resource limitations as well as physical conditions. These conditions, especially resource limitations, affect not only the owner (and possibly the construction manager as well), but also contractors. Consequently, resequencing usually requires the concurrence of those parties. In carrying out resequencing, care must be exercised to avoid adverse consequences, for example, walls being finished before interior wiring is completed.

Comment 10. On-line computer systems which permit the modeling of the effects on costs and on the schedule of alternative sequencing arrangements, are valuable in achieving optimum resequencing. Consequently, newer on-line construction information systems can have advantages over the older batch-mode systems.

Second shifts.

Overtime.

Prefabrication of materials.

Preassembly of materials.

Adding equipment.

Performing operations in parallel.

Comment 11. Physical constraints—the impossibility of too many men working in a tight space, or nonmaneuverability of equipment may preclude parallel operations.

Reducing test periods.

Comment 12. This technique for making up scheduling shortfalls has risks, unless the test periods were set overgenerously to begin with. The "shrinking" invites test shortcuts, the consequence of which could be either acceptance of a substandard structure or, alternatively, a delay in occupancy when the need for additional testing is recognized.

Overall schedule postponcments.

Comment 13. The key consideration in adopting this expedient is whether the postponement will result in a reduction in the flow of revenue, while carrying charges are continuing.

G. As appropriate, checking summary information (point G.1 to detail in G.2) as follows:

Comment 14. The actions prescribed to complete this step are based on the assumption that the results of comprehensive testing of the cost-accumulation system, and of its "feeder" systems, provide additional assurance that all authorized data and only such data is accurately input and updated.

1. By determining whether the appropriate supervisory or management personnel have reviewed and approved documented investigations relating performance monitoring to performance indicators as follows:

    (a) For the budget and other cost-related factors:

    Actual cost to date plus estimated cost to complete versus budget.

    Actual cost versus physical completion.

    Actual material, labor, and overhead costs versus budget to date.

    Cost savings originated to date.

(b) For the construction schedule and other timeliness-related factors:

The actual percentage of completion to date for each structure or area and the project as a whole.

The actual percentage of completion compared to scheduled percentage of completion for each structure or area and the project as a whole.

The impact of delays measured in terms of contractor claims.

> *Comment 15.* The review of claims for delays may affect not only the claimant and the owner but also another contractor if it is found that the latter has caused the claimant's delay.

Contractor overtime (as an indication of slippage against the construction schedule).

Contractor labor productivity.

> *Comment 16.* The actual monitoring of labor productivity is covered by a separate objective; however, the results of such monitoring are relevant to monitoring overall contractor performance.

(c) For qualitative factors, as indicated by the results of the following inspections:

Of materials and equipment at the contractor's plant during manufacturing.

Of the site receiving inspection.

For quality assurance.

2. By examining documented reviews in detail to determine whether they addressed the following points:

(a) The determination of actual costs to date plus estimated costs to complete (noting whether the information on key cost factors such as material prices, labor productivity, and labor rates, is kept up to date).

> *Comment 17.* The calculation of estimated costs to complete may be complex. It should be based on estimates of

work to be performed based on physical inspections supplemented by analyses of drawings, reviews of bills of materials and instructions, etc.; simple deduction of actual costs to date from budget is unlikely to give a satisfactory result.

(b) The determination of actual physical percentage of completion (relying for the investigation primarily on reports of inspections and meetings concerned with the determination, and if appropriate, personal inspection of the construction site).

(c) The comparison of actual material, labor, and overhead to budget to date, as indicated by variances in:

Purchase price, representing the difference between actual and estimated unit price multiplied by units purchased.

Material usage, representing the difference between estimated units to be used and actual units used multiplied by the estimated unit price.

Labor efficiency, representing the difference between estimated labor hours and actual labor hours incurred, multiplied by the estimated unit cost.

Labor cost, representing the difference between actual and estimated labor unit cost, multiplied by the actual labor units used.

Scheduling, representing the difference between costs actually incurred and costs that would have been incurred if the schedule had been adhered to.

Overhead, representing over- or under-absorbed overhead.

(d) All quality inspections, specifically:

Their nature.

The extent of their findings, including the relation of actual to expected quality, rework levels called for, and the relation of actual to expected reject levels.

Their recommendations, the nature of the specific steps planned to implement them, and the extent to which such follow-up plans have been implemented on past recommendations.

(e) Quality control inspections and quality assurance reviews and inspections, as indicated by the level of exceptions found that should have been found during a "lower-level" inspection.

Comment 18. When the level of such exceptions indicates a need for improved lower-level inspection, it may also be desirable to intensify upper-level inspection until the efficiency of lower-level inspection is satisfactory.

3. By determining, through examination of evidence and, if necessary, by questioning personnel and observing procedures directly, whether all contractor-prepared data was checked and, if so, whether the checker was independent of the contractor and the checking was reviewed and approved by appropriate supervisory personnel.

H. Evaluating, for completeness and timeliness, the documentation of monitoring activities, using techniques such as the pay-point system, defined below, for processing computer-generated or standardized forms.

Comment 19. A "pay-point" system creates computer-generated input forms, at predetermined dates or at specified levels of completion, to report physical progress in terms of timeliness and quality. The system can significantly reduce the amount of time spent on paperwork.

I. Looking for any information that might shed further light on performance to date.

J. Determining whether there has been any attempt to identify conditions that could adversely affect a contractor's ability to perform, for example, imminent bankruptcy or overcommitment of resources, and:

1. If such an attempt has been made, determining what actions have been taken in response to adverse findings.

2. Regardless of whether the attempt has been made, conducting an independent investigation designed to uncover such adverse conditions.

Third-Party Reporting Compliance

Objective

Evaluate the external reporting of results to third parties.

Tasks

Review reports to third parties to evaluate the completeness, accuracy, validity, and compliance with applicable regulatory requirements.

> *Comment 1.* The nature, extent, and timing of the following tests may vary in accordance with the monitoring tests of the cost-accumulation system and of reviews of performance against performance indicators. The tests are formulated on the assumption that the results of the monitoring tests show the controls over the completeness, accuracy, authorization, and maintenance of the data summarized into the general ledger to be functioning effectively.

The review and evaluation should involve:

A. Testing the mathematical accuracy of reports.
B. Determining whether report amounts agree with appropriate general ledger accounts and evaluating the propriety of report classifications.
C. Determining whether the report and related disclosures comply with regulatory and tax requirements.

> *Comment 2.* Proper evaluation of tax regulations may result in substantial savings or deferrals of income taxes. For instance, interest capitalized for financial reporting purposes may be currently deductible for income tax purposes and additions to construction in progress may be eligible for investment tax credits, energy credits, or state job development credits.

CHAPTER SEVENTEEN

Final Steps

Comprehensive Start-up Tests and Moving Plans

Objective

Evaluate policies and procedures relative to opening and operating the finished facility.

Tasks

Review policies and established procedures governing testing, occupying, and staffing the new facility (including hiring and training) to assess their comprehensiveness and to determine whether they have been approved by the appropriate parties and whether their implementation is on schedule. The review should include:

A. Determining whether the policies have been reviewed and approved by management.

B. Assessing their coverage of:

    1. Testing.

        Comment 1. The extent of testing varies in accordance with the nature of the facility. In many cases it is only necessary to perform the action indicated on the punch lists that contractors should compile. In other cases, testing should be continued for a significant period after all contractors have left the site.

    2. Moving from the old facility, if appropriate.

      3.   Staffing, as evidenced by preparation of:

         (a)   Organizational charts.

         (b)   Job descriptions for all positions and necessary qualifications.

         (c)   A training calendar for supervisors and staff.

      4.   Pilot operations.

C.   Comparing the approved timetable for implementation of policies and procedures to the latest construction schedule.

D.   Determining, on the basis of information from persons connected with the testing process and with the evaluation of the test results (and any formalities connected with following up these results, such as hearing appeals and evaluating rework) whether these activities were adequately documented.

E.   Determining, on the basis of available documentation and information from persons connected with testing and the evaluation of test results whether:

      1.   The tests were of the appropriate duration, in the right time sequence, directed by persons with the appropriate authority and credentials, continuously controlled and supervised, subject to the follow-up on exceptions, and in all other respects in accord with prescribed procedures.

        Comment 2.   Notice that these requirements are essentially the same as for quality control and quality assurance inspections.

      2.   The evaluation of test results and any subsequent formalities connected with following up this evaluation are in accordance with authorized procedures (or sound business practices) and directed by persons with appropriate authority and credentials.

F.   Evaluating the criteria for selecting the person who coordinated the move.

G.   Reviewing moving plans to determine whether they provide for:

      1.   Items to be moved.

      2.   Physical security during the move.

      3.   Disposal of items not to be moved.

      4.   If appropriate, acquisition of new items to replace items disposed of.

      5.   Distribution of written moving instructions to employees.

H.   Determining whether hiring recommendations at the new facility were reviewed and approved by the appropriate managers and that the recommendations cite sound reasons.

I.   Examining personnel files (i.e., transcripts and reference checks) to determine whether employee qualifications were evaluated and specifics of employment history verified.

J.   Reviewing the training calendar and comparing it to the timetable for the implementation of facility-testing and staff-training policies and procedures and to the construction schedule.

K.   Reviewing the new facility's accounting system to determine whether:

   1.   It reflects the transition from the construction phase to the operational phase.

   2.   Reasonable accounting routines have been created for revenues and expenses during the start-up period.

   3.   Rules of regulatory authorities are being followed.

Project Results Guide Future Planning

Objective

Determine whether project performance was systematically compared to performance indicators and, if so, evaluate the comparison and the use that is being made of it in connection with future projects.

Comment 1. This objective may not be applicable if there are no significant construction projects planned for after the current one.

Tasks

Review the final project performance report to determine whether it has been approved by the appropriate parties and evaluate the report and its supporting documentation for completeness, accuracy, and usefulness. The review and evaluation should involve:

A.   Determining (on the basis of signatures of approval, documentation of the nature and extent of review procedures performed, memoranda relating to questions, and other evidence) whether the overall project performance report and all supporting reviews performed have been reviewed and approved by appropriate levels of management.

B. Reviewing the report and the supporting reviews for clarity and practical recommendations.

C. Examining the report for coverage of the following specific aspects, and, as appropriate, assessing the completeness, accuracy, and relevance of the data on which they are based:

1. Cost:
   (a) By comparing with actual cost both the original budget and the amended budgets, and explaining the following variances:

   Material price.

   > *Comment 2.* Possible corrective actions include improving the estimating process, possibly by seeking future bids from more cost-conscious vendors.

   Material quantity.

   > *Comment 3.* Possible corrective actions include improving control over design, establishing awareness programs to minimize waste, strengthening security over materials, and improving receiving and storage procedures.

   Labor efficiency.

   > *Comment 4.* A battery of remedial options is available, ranging from the recruitment of new labor to improving training and supervision, raising technical qualifications, and stimulating motivation by such means as quality circles (informal yet structured discussions between supervisors and workers aimed at resolving problems in quality or productivity).

   Labor price.

   > *Comment 5.* In general, the remedies for this variance lie in improving *future* assignments and perhaps also in closer control of union negotiations and greater use of open-shop labor.

   Budget or overhead.

Item. An international telecommunications company constructed a new corporate headquarters. However, this company had not updated its procedures pertaining to the computation of the investment tax credit to allow for the latest, liberalized Internal Revenue Service requirements. Consequently, the company was deprived of additional cash flow from maximization of the investment tax credit.

Scheduling.

Comment 6. The remedy for scheduling variances lies in assessing the reasons for shortfalls in scheduling and initiating corrective action.

(b) By comparing cost savings utilized with identifiable cost-saving opportunities.

(c) By determining costs of:
Change-orders.
Scope definitions (i.e., by the architect or engineer).

(d) By comparing the cost of settled claims with amount of asserted claims.

(e) By determining the dollar value of claims not yet settled.

Comment 7. When there are claims that will not be settled for an extended period of time beyond completion of the facility, the time and expense of settling these claims should be considered as a negative factor when evaluating overall project performance.

2. Timeliness:

(a) By comparing with actual completion time both the original schedule and the amended schedules.

Comment 8. An analysis of significant structural components may be appropriate to help evaluate overall project performance in this area.

(b) By comparing time-saving opportunities that were implemented with total time-saving opportunities identified.

3. Quality, by comparing actual project quality to original expected quality.

    D.   Determining whether project problems, including those involving labor relations, public relations, and obtaining permits and licenses, have been analyzed with a view towards corrective action.

    E.   Evaluating, for reasonableness, the analyses of variances and the recommendations for future improvement.

    F.   Determining whether the expectations of the initiators of the project, based on the feasibility study, are being realized in actual practice. Such a "make good" report would cover not only construction performance but also initial and later payback from operations.

Preemptive Auditing: Controlling Construction Costs—Key Activities

INTRODUCTION

In response to frequent construction cost overruns and schedule delays, Coopers & Lybrand developed Preemptive Auditing™—a comprehensive approach to controlling project costs.

Preemptive Auditing is constructive in both intent and execution. It differs from a traditional audit in that a Preemptive Audit is designed to enhance management's decision-making capabilities. On a Preemptive Audit, our experienced staff members review the owner's project management techniques and identify opportunities for additional cost savings.

Preemptive Auditing is normally performed in two nondiscrete phases: the design/engineering phase and the construction/compliance phase. Members of our Preemptive Auditing team are involved with a project from its inception through its completion. Throughout an engagement, we stress auditing *before* any money is spent—or even committed—and we continuously monitor the construction effort.

The outline that follows describes key activities performed as part of a Preemptive Audit. Although these activities apply to most major construction projects, this outline is *not* all inclusive.

DESIGN/ENGINEERING PHASE

Project Plan

Review the project plan to make certain it includes:

A description of the work to be accomplished.

A cost estimate.

A timetable for completion.

Assignments for managing all project functions.

A philosophy toward construction. (For example, will the work be performed directly by the owner or the construction manager, or will contractors handle it?)

A philosophy toward contracted work. (Will fixed-price contracts or cost-reimbursable contracts be used?)

Provisions for having these activities reviewed by the appropriate management levels.

Organizational Structure

Determine that an organizational structure has been developed and approved. Review this structure to see that it:

Will help attain the project's objectives.

Ensures proper coverage of all key internal and external functions.

Provides for clear reporting relationships.

Promotes the cost-effective use of personnel.

Will make sure qualified technical personnel are employed.

Design/Engineering Function

Review the design/engineering function to make certain:

All work activities are defined.

Responsibility for all work activities is assigned to the appropriate qualified personnel.

Work is being properly coordinated and is proceeding efficiently.

All design activities include provisions for operations and maintenance, as well as for construction.

Construction Management Tasks

Review how construction management tasks are defined and how they are assigned to see whether:

The appropriate parties have been consulted so that tasks are more completely identified.

Tasks are assigned to persons with the requisite capability and authority to successfully complete them.

Performance Indicators

Set up performance indicators to measure cost, timeliness, and quality before construction starts. Be sure to:

Establish intermediate checkpoints for comparing actual costs, quantities, or events to those planned or budgeted.

Use trend charts or other measurements to see how the units installed or the man-hours required per unit compare to initial expectations.

Review inspection reports, test results, and exceptions to standards to determine whether quality objectives are being met.

Licensing and Regulatory Requirements

Identify all licensing and regulatory requirements and set up a system to ensure that all requirements are complied with on a timely basis. Some of the major requirements include:

Environmental issues.

Zoning laws.

Engineering standards.

Affirmative Action/Equal Employment Opportunities.

Major Project Risks

Identify the major risks to the project, such as strikes, labor shortages, inflation, late delivery of materials, licensing problems, or adverse weather conditions. Determine whether these risks should be:

Assumed by the owner.
Transferred to another party, such as the contractor.
Insured against the probability of their occurrence.
Managed so their impact is reduced.
Controlled through a combination of these methods.

Budget

Review the project's budget, paying particular attention to the:

Methods used to estimate costs.
Assumptions underlying the budget.
Actual costs of similar, recently completed structures.
Method used to determine escalation rates.
Determination of the contingency amount.
Accuracy of quantity estimates.
Labor productivity estimates.
Overhead allocation estimates.

Schedule

Review the project schedule, paying particular attention to the:

Construction and procurement schedule.
Methods and assumptions used to develop the schedule.
Parties reviewing and/or approving various schedules.
Reasonableness and frequency of schedule updates.
Time it took to complete similar projects.

Quality Control

Discuss the level of quality control desired with the project manager. Be sure to:

Determine whether a project quality control manual exists.

Review quality control policies to make sure they will allow objectives to be met.

Determine whether any special training requirements have been identified.

Examine policies covering work areas that are sensitive to construction failures, such as concrete, steel, or formwork.

Review the effectiveness of quality control inspections.

Examine quality control forms and output to determine if they are enhancing efficiency or merely generating unnecessary paperwork.

Project Coordination

Make sure that proper project coordination exists between all appropriate internal and external parties, including:,

Owner departments.

Architect/engineer.

Construction manager/general contractors.

Other construction contractors.

Other project consultants.

Management Information System

Review the project's management information system. Determine its ability to adequately control and report on the project's progress, cost, and schedule. Make certain that:

All user needs are identified.

The reports needed to properly control the project are identified.

A computerized system is really needed.

The proper hardware and software are selected.

Plans to implement and operate the system are developed.

Contract Administration

Review contract administration activities, checking the:

Adequacy of the contract administration organization.

Adequacy of standard contract clauses.

Process for developing and reviewing bid packages.

Process for documenting any contract administration policies and procedures.

Contractor Selection

Review all contractor selection activities, including:

Bidder prequalification practices.

Bidder's lists.

Bid evaluation practices.

Controls over post-bid negotiations.

Contract execution activities.

CONSTRUCTION/COMPLIANCE PHASE

Document Control

Review job-site document control activities to:

Make sure that copies of all construction contracts and related documents are transferred to the field office.

Verify that the latest revisions to drawings, specifications, and other technical documents are being received and properly controlled and distributed to field personnel.

Determine that the drawings and specifications used for construction have been properly approved.

Check the file system's organization, its effectiveness, and the retrievability of documents.

Control of Claims and Change-Orders

Determine that adequate procedures exist for controlling claims and processing change-orders by:

Making sure claims are quickly and accurately reviewed by the appropriate field personnel.

Determining that any extra work performed on a cost-plus basis is closely monitored.

Recommending modifications to work practices that would help claims control.

Reviewing procedures for processing change-orders to make certain all charges are accurate and have been approved by the proper person.

Materials Procurement

Review the field materials procurement function to make certain:

Materials and equipment are being obtained at competitive prices.

Adequate procedures exist for effective field procurement control.

Procurement schedules provide sufficient lead time to support construction needs.

Costs are being charged to the proper accounts.

Field requisition practices are in order.

Materials Management

Review the materials management function to make certain adequate controls exist in these areas:

Receiving and inspection.

Expediting.

Storage requirements.

Recordkeeping.

Accounting and inventory control.

Surplus materials disposal.

Labor Productivity

If portions of the work are performed on a cost-plus basis, review the labor productivity monitoring effort to make certain it includes:

Documentation of employee attendance.

A means of determining if work is being performed efficiently.

Suggestions on how to improve labor productivity on the site.

A comparison of actual productivity rates to scheduled productivity indicators.

AA/EEO Compliance

Monitor compliance with any established Affirmative Action/Equal Employment Opportunity guidelines, including:

Adherence to specific goals or targets.

Progress by contractor or by major activity.

Ability to implement an effective minority program.

Cost Accumulation and Control

Determine that effective cost-accumulation policies and procedures exist and that they include provisions for:

Reviewing and approving invoices.

Accounting for all transactions that affect construction costs.

Reviewing account codings.

Accurately posting cost-accumulation records for all project costs.

Reviewing all contract-retention practices and all retention-release procedures.

Reporting Systems

Review the job-site reporting systems to make certain:

All pertinent construction activities and problems are included in periodic progress reports to management.

Reports that will help field supervisory personnel control various functions are generated.

Contractor Performance

Determine whether an effective system for monitoring and evaluating contractor performance has been established. Make certain this system allows for:

Verifying compliance with contract provisions.

Monitoring contractor costs and comparing them to cost performance indicators and to the budget.

Measuring actual performance against the construction schedule.

Monitoring actual performance for compliance with quality control procedures.

Evaluating overall contractor performance after work is completed.

ADDITIONAL PREEMPTIVE AUDITING ACTIVITIES

Because Preemptive Auditing is, by its very nature, flexible, additional activities may be added, depending on the needs of an individual project. There may be situations where a project owner may want other tasks performed, either during the design/engineering phase or during the construction/compliance phase. These additional activities, which are summarized below, often become part of a Preemptive Audit engagement.

Design/Engineering Phase

During this phase, a Preemptive Audit can also include either—or both—of these steps:

Review the feasibility and site selection studies to ensure that the cost/benefit of all available alternatives to construction and all possible sites have been investigated before going ahead with construction.

Review project financing considerations to ensure that all alternatives (e.g., own the project outright, pursue a sale/lease-back arrangement, mortgage the property or obtain bank financing) have been appropriately evaluated before selecting the financing arrangement.

Construction/Compliance Phase

While construction is in progress, a Preemptive Audit can also include any—or all—of these steps:

Review site security provisions to see if they adequately and economically protect against theft and other related losses.

Evaluate project safety practices for their effectiveness in eliminating work-related accidents and for their cost effectiveness.

Evaluate construction equipment procurement policies and related financing practices to make certain that procurement is properly coordinated with the construction schedule and that these policies minimize total equipment costs.

Review temporary construction support facilities with management to see that these services are in accordance with contract conditions.

Evaluate labor relations practices for their effectiveness in maximizing productivity while reducing the number of labor disruptions and work stoppages.

Review the facility testing and start-up operations and go over the move-in coordination efforts to make sure they are timely and effective.

Preemptive Auditing: Controlling Construction Costs

CONSTRUCTION OWNER'S CHECKLIST

Introduction

The subject checklist should be of interest to clients engaged in relatively discontinuous construction, of a noncomplex nature. This type of client is less likely to have a construction management team in place than a client in an industry where there is constant renewal of facilities.

The objectives in the checklist are the objectives of the client. He may use an arsenal of techniques, singly or in combination, to achieve the objectives. Generally, there should be evidence that the techniques have been emplaced and are functioning.

If techniques have not been installed that offer a likelihood that the objectives will be achieved, the client may be confronted by adverse consequences in terms of cost overruns, schedule delays, or quality deficiencies.

I. Arrange for a *feasibility study* to be conducted by persons of professional stature, to contribute to an informed "go/no go" decision, based on the perceived costs and benefits of a proposed project.

Comment. In general, the study should show the acquisition costs of the proposed project and the revenues and costs estimated to result upon its completion. The study should also present under-lying assumptions, *inter alia* relative to project size, timing, quality, design, and risk.

II.   *Select a site* based on consideration of available alternatives, if any.

Comment.   Site selection will be influenced by the following:

Proximity to markets.

Proximity to raw materials.

Proximity to transportation.

Proximity to sources of energy.

Real and personal property tax aspects.

Quality of life.

Availability of labor and nature of the labor relations prevailing in the community.

III.   Define approach to *risk management*.

Comment.   This step requires identification of the risks that may affect the project—for example, labor stoppages, energy shortages, and inflation—together with a determination of the approach taken to manage risk.

In essence, risk may be disregarded, shifted to others, or reduced via control, or a combination of approaches. To the extent that risk will be controlled through the system, the required modifications will need to be made.

IV.   *Select architect.*

Comment.   The architect's initial work involves preparation of preliminary drawings, together with a preliminary cost estimate. The design represents an important device for controlling costs; any major modifications should be subjected to cost/benefit evaluation.

Selection of an architect involves balancing of cost against the architect's professional skills. Attention should be given to the reputations of individuals proposed to be assigned to the en-gagement and to the extent to which their time is being committed. It may be advantageous to verify asserted achievements by direct contact with prior clients.

V.   Establish a *realistic budget*.

    Comment.   The budget involves:

    Realistic prices for materials, based on recent prices, and on current and foreseeable escalation.

    Labor costs based on drawing quantities, realistic productivity, current wage rates, and current and foreseeable escalation.

    Overhead based on dedication of individuals to the engagement, together with realistic allocations of overhead.

    Contingencies for design and construction, and of a general nature.

VI.   *Arrange financing*.

    Comment.   Depending on the nature of the project and on borrowing power, an owner may fully own a project, he may pursue a sale/lease-back arrangement, the property may be mortgaged, or a variety of combination financing arrangements may be followed. Since each approach has advantages and disadvantages, the optimum approach should be based upon guidance from financial/tax advisors.

VII.   Decide on approach to *construction management*.

    Comment. Construction management may be performed by the owner, construction manager, or general contractor. Each choice has advantages and disadvantages. If an owner manages construction, he will need to bring aboard individuals with requisite skills. This approach is costly for owners with discontinuous construction. The general contractor arrangement is suitable for construction of a relatively "cut and dried" variety; some general contractors may base their decisions on their own interest, rather than that of the owner.

    The construction management approach brings the judgment of an independent professional to project control. However, this approach may involve fees, and incentives, to the construction manager. Safeguards must be introduced to ensure that compensation to him is based upon the value of services and not the achievement of targets set solely by the construction manager.

VIII. Establish realistic *construction schedules,* linked to the funding plan.

Comment.   Different approaches to scheduling are available:

A straight time sequenced approach.

A critical path management approach; identification is made of items having the longest lead times, or the greatest importance relative to the balance of the structure; "critical path" items are given special surveillance.

Fast-tracking or modified fast-tracking; rather than complete design and construction sequentially, construction starts as soon as drawings are completed for a particular section, while drawings are still in preparation for other sections.

The choice of approach depends upon the owner's needs to complete the project, availability of materials and labor, and capacity for control. Once an approach has been selected, schedules must be developed, and appropriately coordinated, and physical progress monitored.

The construction schedule and the financing plan must be integrated. The owner may have a choice of drawing immediately on monies for the entire project, or taking down funds as contractor billings come through. If the entire proceeds are taken down immediately, provision should be made for temporary investment of unneeded funds, usually via secured loans. (If the take-down is based on construction progress, banks will charge a relatively nominal "standby" fee.)

IX.   Select *contract policies* to shift uncertainties to contractors insofar as possible, but without discouraging bids or inviting inflated prices; also incentives should be included in contracts to spur performance.

Comment.   Essentially, contracts may be of the following major types or of combinations thereof:

Lump-sum—the contract is for a fixed amount including overhead and profit.

Unit-price. The contract sets a price (either fixed or "sliding") for each of an established number of units; overrun or underrun provisions may exist explicitly or implicitly; there may or may not exist an overall quantity or dollar cap.

Cost-plus-fixed-fee. The contractor charges actual cost, plus a fee for his services; the fee may or may not depend upon the value of costs; the fee may or may not include incentive provisions; the fee may or may not be subject to an overall cap.

Contract policies are subject to local legal requirements, they may be affected by the nature of the project, and by demand/supply. The approach should be selected on the basis of professional study. The owner's rights should be safeguarded, and savings/incentive technique adopted.

X. See to compliance with *minority business enterprise* (MBE) rules and affirmative action requirements.

Comment. Compliance with MBE rules may involve quotas set for contract value, number of contracts, and/or number of minority workers.

The approach should be based upon meaning to the minority community, and upon a company's capacity and willingness to achieve its plan. Key aspects involve:

Goals setting given reasonable parameters and realistic "stretch."

Sourcing.

Up-front training of minority employees.

Monitoring of MBE performance to detect shortfalls.

Creation of objective fact-gathering mechanisms.

Reporting against goals.

XI. Create a system for *selecting vendors competitively.*

Comment. Vendors should be prequalified on the basis of prior cost, quality, and delivery performances. Where experience does not exist, the award should be based upon investigation of the potential vendor's equipment, shop facilities—if pertinent— financial capability, supervisory capacity, and record on projects of a similar nature. Contact with prior customers should involve individuals other than those whose names have been given for reference.

Normally, awards should be based primarily on cost, although it may be desirable to rate less tangible factors. The evaluations should proceed along reasonably objective lines. Key steps involve:

Selection of vendors eligible to receive bidding invitations.

Mailing of comprehensive bid packages including "pro forma" terms and technical and general specifications.

Prebid conferences.

Award to the appparent low bidder—subject to exception routines and controls.

Monitoring of post-award negotiations to insure that the objectives of competitive bidding will not be vitiated.

XII.   Install a system for *monitoring construction* in progress to ensure that deviations from cost, quality, and delivery targets are flagged in a timely manner as a basis to corrective action.

Comment. The owner may choose to delegate systems details to the construction manager and rely on his reports—such an approach is perilous unless reinforced by owner monitoring.

In general, systems should be computerized, rather than manual, unless construction is of a simple type and a traditional cost ledger, broken down by structural components/contracts is adequate.

Physical progress of a project should be measured and compared to financial progress. Measurement is inherent in the following formula: Cost-to-date plus estimated cost to complete equals total projected cost; total projected cost less budget equals budget underrun/overrun.

Construction systems must interface with other corporate systems.

An indication of timeliness of physical progress can be obtained as follows: Contract value multiplied by days elapsed from the beginning of construction to the measurement date divided by total days from the beginning of construction to scheduled completion. The result may be regarded as cost that should have been incurred had the time schedule been achieved. Cost computed less costs paid indicates the scheduling shortfalls/overage.

XIII.   Establish a *contractor coordination* system.

Comment. Such a system should insure, via scheduled meetings and exchange of written information, that problems are identified early on. Typically, contractor claims are based on assertions that delays were created by activities not subject to claimant's control; claims may also be asserted as a result of faulty work and/or rework allegedly caused by the owner, other contractors, or inadequate design; claims may also be entered for unforeseen conditions. The owner or his representative must monitor claims assertions to insure that reasonable steps are taken to minimize damage, insofar as practical, and that parties are treated equitably.

Contractor complaints and/or claims are disregarded by owners at their own risk. Unchallenged claims acquire cachet simply by not being challenged.

XIV.   *Monitor construction.*

Comment.   The owner should visit the site to ensure that activities reported as taking place are actually in progress. Observations of workers, and assessments of their productivity, may be pertinent even if contracts are for a fixed price; extensive idleness by workers could indicate that the contracts were entered into on a disadvantageous cost basis, or that various loading or unbalancing approaches were applied by contractors.

Attention should be given to engineering changes, usually triggered by design "definition" or changes, regulatory or legal considerations, changes resulting from unforeseen events, or changes resulting from claims.

In general, changes should be examined to determine whether they are in-scope—in which case the contractor is responsible for them—or out-of-scope, in which case the change is for the owner's account. If changes involve significant sums, consideration should be given to competitive bidding, if practical. Further, changes should also be considered in the light of available alternatives, if any.

XV.   Appoint *move coordinator.*

Comment.   Responsibilities of the move coordinator include:

Integration of move-related activities of the architect, construction manager, general contractor, and mover.

Determination of which assets are to be left behind at the old facilities and which are to be moved.

Procurement of new equipment on a timely basis to ensure availability when needed to commence operations at the new facility.

Cost-effective disposal of surplus equipment.

Equipment identification, scheduling, routing, and dispatching to ensure that the move proceeds in a cost-effective manner and with minimal disruption of operations.

Preemptive Auditing: Controlling Construction Costs

CONSTRUCTION MANAGEMENT RESPONSIBILITIES

Construction management vitally affects planning, design, and construction. The function involves direction, supervision, coordination, and review, all for the purpose of completing a project of acceptable quality within budget, and on schedule.

There is no generally accepted list of construction management responsibilities. Consequently, such responsibilities must be defined in writing. If construction management responsibilities are transferred to others by an owner, performance of the agreed-upon responsibilities should be evidenced, reported, and subject to owner oversight and monitoring. Moreover, in order to strengthen control an owner may find it advantageous to divide construction management responsibilities between an outside construction manager, the owner's staff, and an outside independent "controller." Regardless of the details of the arrangement, the owner should stay involved, and his involvement should be active and documented. I have developed a list of construction management responsibilities which, while it is broad, is not necessarily all-inclusive. Hopefully, it will be of value in deciding upon an approach to construction management responsibilities, and in tailoring those responsibilities to the needs of the situation.

Systems and Procedures

Accounting control system reflecting budgeted cost of each function, contract, or significant component based on a definitive estimate, together with actual cost and latest cost to complete, as well as explanations of variances and recommended managerial actions.

Current status reports including projected activities, performance against prior period projections, cash-flow projections, and contact commitments.

Reports, directives, and other data intended to assist the owner, and others with a need to know, in project administration and in compliance with state, federal, and local laws.

Procedures, preferably in the form of a written manual covering operating instructions, forms, and input documents, together with output reports and schedules.

Master schedule establishing major project milestones for planning, design, construction, and fitting out, including appropriate lead times.

Records, appropriately maintained, of contracts, shop drawings, subcontracts, machine operating instructions, maintenance handbooks, etc.

EDP services relating to the project cost accounts, CPM schedules, and to related subsystems such as payrolls, procurement records, and accounts payable, etc.

Planning and Design

Risk analysis.

Project cost model.

Periodic cost projections coordinated with project progress.

Assistance in determining licensing requirements and in being responsive to such requirements.

Review of the conceptual design and of related documents, giving weight to the impact of materials on construction techniques and on cost, quality, and delivery.

In consultation with the architect, the interpretation of design modifications and of drawing refinements.

Procedures for creating, expediting, issuing, and controlling shop drawings.

Procurement

Assistance in the development of contractual policies.

Assistance and recommendations pertaining to the contents of the "pro forma" contract, or "bid package."

Assistance with respect to broad bid solicitations.

Prequalification criteria for bidders and suppliers.

Review of bidder qualifications, including shop inspections.

Attendance at the prebid conference.

Review of bids and proposals; recommendations pertaining to awards.

Assistance in the selection of consultants and specialty contractors.

Expediting.

Receiving.

Storage and materials handling.

Assistance with traffic management at the construction site and externally.

Construction

Coordination, supervision, administration, and direction of contractors.

Measurements of labor productivity when appropriate.

Review and processing of progress payment applications to ensure they are being based on work actually accomplished and in conformance to contracts.

Conduct of contractor coordination meetings.

Observation and/or measurement of labor productivity.

Initiation of recommendations for project changes, giving appropriate consideration to the cost, scheduling, and quality impact.

Cost analyses and technical reviews of contractor-recommended changes, including drawings and specifications, together with preparation of recommendations.

Assistance in connection with contract or drawing interpretations.

Assistance relative to claims asserted or actions brought by contractors relative to design or construction, including the preparation of recommendations.

Tests and observations to ensure appropriate quality of construction.

Inspection followed by acceptance or rejection of contractor's work based on appropriate quality standards and on contract conformance.

Review of unsettled claims together with recommendations.

Cost audits.

Other

Provision of project office facilities.

Provision of power.

Cleaning, maintenance, and pest control services.

Security services.

Supervision, administration, and coordination of equipment installation.

Building permits and special permits.

Preparation of occupancy schedules.

Coordination of contractor-shared facilities.

Preoperation check of utilities, operating systems, and similar equipment.

Achievement of a climate of understanding and goodwill with regulatory agencies, unions, contractors, and the community.

Administration of equal opportunity and affirmative action programs.

Installation and operation of safety programs.

Selection and training of maintenance personnel.

Final inspection and acceptance or rejection of the work together with appropriate recommendations.

Preemptive Auditing: Controlling Construction Costs

SAVINGS OPPORTUNITIES

Preemptive Auditing: Controlling Construction Costs–Savings Opportunities

SPECIFIC BENEFITS

Techniques	Protect quality	Keep to schedule	Comply with laws	Contain inflation	Optimize cash utilization/debt management	Stop unfavorable trends	Cut material costs	Cut labor costs	Cut overhead/C/M fees	Cut freight	Improve equipment utilization	Limit scope changes/claims	Cut scrap
1. Establish criteria for evaluating program effectiveness "up front."													
2. Set executive performance standards which require "stretch."													
3. Conduct feasibility study: select optimum financing approaches.					$								
4. Study alternate sites and make optimum selection.						$							
5. Maintain active oversight.						$	$	$	$				
6. See that no vital planning/design/construction functions remain unassigned.									$				
7. Consider the information needs of all concerned in establishing the reporting structure.													

8. Control engineering/consulting efforts via defined tasks, specified deliverables, and realistic timetables.

9. Ensure constructibility.

10. Secure nonstrike agreements from operating/construction unions.

11. Conform to present and anticipated regulatory requirements.

12. Select optimum contracting approach.

13. Shift risk to vendors and others to the degree possible.

14. Offer shared savings incentives to vendors and others.

15. Cap material and labor contracts.

16. Recognize savings opportunities.

17. Document budget assumptions.

18. Set rational contingencies.

19. Integrate schedule and cost control; incorporate modeling attributes.

20. Prequalify vendors insofar as possible.

21. Incorporate needed administrative and clerical lead time in schedules.

Item	C1	C2	C3	C4	C5	C6	C7	C8	C9	C10	C11	C12	C13
8			$		$	$	$						
9		$				$	$						
10		$			$	$	$						
11		$		$	$	$	$						$
12	$	$			$	$	$				$		
13	$	$	$	$	$	$	$			$			$
14	$		$	$	$	$	$			$			
15	$												
16			$	$	$	$	$						
17						$	$						$
18													
19													
20						$							
21						$	$						$

Preemptive Auditing: Controlling Construction Costs—Savings Opportunities

SPECIFIC BENEFITS

Techniques	Protect quality	Keep to schedule	Comply with laws	Contain inflation	Optimize cash utilization/debt management	Stop unfavorable trends	Cut material costs	Cut labor costs	Cut overhead/C/M fees	Cut freight	Improve equipment utilization	Limit scope changes/claims	Cut scrap
22. Standardize on preferred items.	$						$						
23. Utilize value analysis.	$						$						
24. Focus on life-cycle costs.	$						$						
25. Conduct focused "shopping."							$						
26. Evaluate bids, considering front-end loading.							$	$	$				
27. Review contractor overhead; establish audit rights.								$	$	$	$	$	$
28. Control post-award negotiations.							$	$	$				
29. Select software, and subsequently hardware, based on performance criteria.	$	$							$				
30. Allow for appropriate systems interfaces.									$				

	C1	C2	C3	C4	C5	C6	C7
31. Cap software costs.					$		
32. Create quality control and assurance routines.	$						
33. Control drawing and other document distribution.	$						
34. Arrange for handling and physical safeguarding of materials.			$	$	$		
35. See to site/data security							
36. Monitor vendor cost, quality, and time compliance.	$	$	$	$	$		
37. Monitor labor productivity.			$	$			
38. Evaluate cost, time, and quality effects of scope and other engineering changes.		$	$		$		
39. Limit claims by early recognition, management, and control.					$	$	
40. Monitor warranty services.	$				$	$	
41. Appoint move expeditor.		$					

$ = Recorded savings

Managing Construction Projects

Introduction

This guide is designed as a tool to help contractors control costs by improving efficiency. It is not a primer of construction management, but rather a series of recommendations aimed at helping managers and field supervisors overcome certain deficiencies in policy and procedure that years of experience have taught us are common in the construction industry. The topics covered include planning, estimating, and scheduling; issuance and distribution of drawings; purchasing and contract administration; management of receiving and storage; and timekeeping and control of equipment.

It cannot be overemphasized that these recommendations should be considered early in the planning process. Even though most of them cannot be implemented until much later, implementation would be difficult if not impracticable unless the administrative groundwork were already laid.

PLANNING AND ESTIMATING

Formal Plan

Virtually all construction jobs of any consequence require a formal, written, "master" plan. It may be possible to do without this plan with a simple project; with large, highly complex projects, such as a paper mill or an atomic power plant, playing it by ear invites disaster. The plan starts with the designing and the engineering of the job. But it must go beyond blueprinting to take in all supporting activities, notably acquiring, storing, and distributing materials, and assembling and supervising a labor force. These activities involve myriad considerations, including estimating, scheduling, and establishing an administrative apparatus.

Documented Facts

The basis of all planning is the efficient gathering and processing of information. "Information" means documented facts, not guesses or unsupported assumptions. The danger of relying on assumptions was brought home painfully not long ago to a builder who specializes in large projects. When the firm was asked to bid on a processing plant, management decided that it could dispense with the usual detailed study and base its estimate on the cost of an *apparently* similar development that the firm had completed some years before. The firm got the contract, but in the end management had no reason to rejoice over the fact. When the firm completed the project, it found that its original estimate, $50 million, had been exceeded by 400 percent. It seems that the similarity between the two projects was superficial. The new structure incorporated technological advances not in the old structure and also required different systems approaches. It is significant, though not surprising, that the builder never attempted to tie suppliers to bids. Management knew that it would have great difficulty in getting bids without providing documentation for bidders, especially drawings and bills of materials. As it turned out, the estimate was so far off that even if some vendors had bid, it is doubtful whether they could have been held to compliance.

On the other hand, where there are supporting documents, care must be taken not to draw specifications too tightly. One company that fabricated cabinets for government-sponsored housing mailed out bid solicitations with specifications far more stringent than required by the Federal Housing Administration. Several qualified vendors refused to bid; the company that finally took the job was inexperienced and proved unable to perform in accordance with the specifications.

Realistic Estimates

The three main elements in estimates are cost of materials, cost of labor, and overhead. Deriving the second element has proven to be a stumbling block in many cases. One company, which custom builds large condensers, could not understand why its estimated costs for producing a particular item bore no relationship to the actual costs. Investigation showed marked inaccuracy in the estimation of labor costs. When overhead percentages were applied to direct labor, the error was multiplied and the estimates grossly distorted. The differential between estimated and actual labor costs was traceable to the fact that the estimators used a higher speed in their calculations than the one at which the machines were actually running.

In this example, the speed of the machines was the major factor in productivity. The less mechanized the operation the greater the importance of labor, as opposed to machine, productivity in the estimates and the greater the significance of quantitative measures of labor productivity. (See below, *Labor and Equipment*, "Productivity Measurement.")

Stated Assumptions

In making estimates it is considered good practice to spell out major assumptions on which estimates are based, that is, period for which funds must be borrowed, interest rate, etc. In that way, if the estimates are not met, it will be possible to identify the causes and to take corrective measures.

Flexibility

Estimates must incorporate provision for changes in costs and must be subject to a post-completion audit at which a determination is made whether performance was adequate in the light of the estimates. If not, planning techniques or performance monitoring must be improved.

Detailed Scheduling

A construction scheduling system must be comprehensive and detailed. A system that is concerned only with construction per se and excludes design, the creating of drawings, purchasing, or the preparation of operating manuals and preoperational testing is incomplete. The system should cover not only the major activities but also the network of subsidiary activities behind each. It is important to adjust the schedule to reflect changes. This principle is sometimes overlooked with regard to the subsidiary activities. Since these may be constantly changing (with the adoption of new methods and materials), this oversight can result in a dangerously obsolete schedule. Where possible, a scheduling system should be linked to cost budgets. While many construction companies have elaborate and well conceived systems for both scheduling and budgeting, the two are not always connected or connectible.

In estimating time required for completing a construction activity, builders typically allow for contingencies, including bad weather. If this is done, it is imperative to account for these factors as separate activities. Otherwise, there is no way of identifying them, and the performance of the contractor in relation to schedules becomes obscured.

Training in Use of Scheduling System

Any scheduling system must be suitable for "firing line" control, that is, for use by the people actually engaged in construction, such as, engineers, foremen, etc. Companies should assume the responsibility for training these people in scheduling; certain builders have even made training available to personnel of subcontractors. Companies willing to do this should stipulate that only persons it approves are eligible; otherwise such contractors might send people who do not qualify as firing line supervisors.

Follow-up training sessions should be conducted methodically and according to a plan (not necessarily formal) of instruction. What can happen when this principle is ignored is illustrated by the experience of an engineering firm that undertook to brief subcontractor personnel in an effort to introduce urgently needed flexibility into its schedule. The sessions were conducted weekly by a project engineer who was supposed to review the previous week's performance and to adjust the activities for the following week. The trouble was that the home office, evidently viewing travel as a burdensome chore, sent a different man each week. Predictably, results were unsatisfactory.

DRAWINGS

Drawings are essential to procurement. Where there are no drawings, there is no basis for making a firm price bid. (Some vendors will decline altogether to submit bids. Others will try to function on the basis of a letter of intent until drawings are delivered or will attempt to negotiate a cost-plus contract.)

Efficiency in the production and distribution of drawings requires a broad approach, with full consideration of interrelated structures and activities.

This approach is implemented by controls over (1) creation of drawings, (2) their modification and updating, and (3) their issuance and return.

The number of drawings that will be needed is an important consideration in planning a project. In estimating this number, it is important to consider the relationship between structures. Failure to do so virtually guarantees that more drawings will ultimately be needed than would otherwise have been the case. One company that ignored structural relationships in estimating the number of drawings for a sophisticated project eventually had to produce 40,000 instead of the 12,000 originally planned on. Some drawings had as many as 25 changes.

Control over Drawing Creation

Unnecessary drawings can be costly. If the superfluous drawings are not utilized, the loss will be confined to the cost of producing them. If they are implemented, the loss can of course be more serious. The following example is instructive even though it is not taken from the construction industry. A large user of varied, heavy packaging employed the services of an engineer "borrowed" from a carton manufacturer to prepare carton drawings. The engineer produced a separate drawing for every variation in size or shape, no matter how insignificant, whereas most of these minor variations could easily have been accommodated by filler pieces at slight cost. As it was, the creation of many different types of cartons led to numerous purchases of small quantities at high unit costs. When the practice was finally stopped the toll had reached $400,000.

Modification of drawings requires advance consideration of the expenses that might be involved in implementing the changes. If the changes call for eliminating any materials that are already on hand, there is a possibility that the no-longer-needed supplies will have to be discarded or sold at little better than scrap prices. Unless these materials can be employed elsewhere by the builder or returned to the vendor, a significant write-off can be anticipated. In one large project, a $100 million foundry, the cost value of materials relegated to the obsolete category was $100,000. In another project, 30 percent completed, the value of discarded materials was $50,000. With amounts like these at stake, it is easy to understand how changes that might be perfectly justifiable in that they make use of cheaper materials feasible, may still be economically ill-advised.

Once the drawings and specifications are produced they must be identified with a code number and the date of issue, as well as the date and code of the superseded drawing (if any).

Issuance and Return

Controls over issuance and return of drawings are sometimes referred to as library controls. The person in charge of the library function must see to it that drawings reach those who need them as soon as possible and that superseded drawings are recalled and replace promptly. Thus he or she must know which items are available and which are outstanding and with whom. This, of course, requires meticulous recordkeeping, a function which, it is stressed, cannot be carried out effectively, unless access to the drawings is restricted. One firm made it a practice to reproduce all drawings in runs of 15 or 20 and to place them in bins on the floor of the construction area where virtually anybody could get at them. With this arrangement there was no way of knowing exactly who had the drawings and therefore it was impossible to recall and replace the superseded ones with any degree of efficiency. Trouble was inevitable and came in due course when extensive foundations were poured in accordance with drawings that had been superseded by a significantly modified version.

An astonishing example of laxity in library controls was furnished by a firm with headquarters in the Northeast. In dispatching vital drawings 2,500 miles to a project site, the home office (1) enclosed under the same cover the only copy of the master record that showed what plans were sent, and (2) failed to notify the addressee that the package was on the way. When the package went astray, nothing was done, since the senders assumed it had arrived and the intended recipients had no knowledge of it.

In some organizations the library function includes administration of drawing reproduction. This involves making sure that no unauthorized copies are produced and that operations are carried out with a maximum of economy and efficiency. (Unsuitable equipment, poor scheduling of print runs, and failure to salvage silver from reproducing solutions are some of the deficiencies commonly encountered in the reproduction operation.)

Numbering System

A mainstay of the systems approach to creating and distributing drawings is the employment of a technologically oriented numbering system that will distinguish drawings on the basis of their contents. Without this kind of a code (which may be highly sophisticated) control over the movements of drawings and over drawing changes is severely handicapped.

PURCHASING

Written Procedures

In a large construction job an overall approach to purchasing is imperative. A syllabus of purchasing procedures should be prepared, defining objectives, assigning responsibilities, laying down criteria for measuring the effectiveness of the purchasing activity, and establishing channels of communication. Assignment of responsibilities is particularly important. In some organizations purchasing is carried on by as many as four different parties, the purchasing department, engineers (responsible, subject to sound purchasing policies, for items of a technical nature), job site personnel, and subcontractors. If the jurisdictions of these purchasing agents are not clearly defined, there is a possibility that they will compete with one another on certain items, raising prices and duplicating purchases.

The reporting line of the purchasing function should be high. In general, where the function is important, overall responsibility should be entrusted to someone on the level of vice-president.

Professional Purchasing

A purchasing agent must be skilled at negotiation and thoroughly familiar with the product he is buying, its properties or function and its price and availability. He must know his organization's need for the product, which of course means that he must understand the exact way in which it is to be used. Ordinarily, purchasing agents should not be instructed to buy particular brands. This policy ties their hands and prevents them from exercising their skill in getting the best price.

Measuring Purchasing Performance

Purchasing performance can be measured in terms of cost or other quantitative criteria. For cost measurement an up-to-date standard cost sheet should be useful. A purchase order, reflecting prices and with variances monitored by management, can be helpful for this purpose. For quantitative measurement of performance, published standards pertaining to the operation of a purchasing department are available. These standards provide guidelines for determining how many requisitions should be processed, how many purchase orders placed, etc.

Specifications

Specifications for items to be purchased are fundamental to the purchasing operation. The specifications must be precise and explicit. If carelessly drafted, they can cause costly errors. One company that designs industrial air conditioning systems bought sheet steel in standard sizes without taking into account the measurements of the end product. As a result, 18 percent of the raw steel value had to be scrapped. With the proper specifications the loss rate could probably have been kept to about 6 percent.

Another company purchased $50,000 worth of gloves for a large construction project. Perhaps because gloves are a small article, nobody attached any importance to them. No attempt was made to prescribe the glove best suited for a particular task; various supervisors were allowed to stipulate their preferences for types and grades. Prices went as high as $25 a dozen pair, although it was possible to obtain a quantity of a serviceable pattern for as little a $3.50 a dozen. (In addition, no notice was taken of the excessive volume of ordering that, as was later shown, resulted from widespread waste and misuse of the gloves.) To curb losses of this sort, the company set up a task force in the purchasing department to identify high-priority targets for cost reduction, article by article. When this policy was extended to 40 different commodities, the dollar savings were significant indeed.

Value Analysis

Value analysis is an important purchasing technique. It can be quite technical, but basically its purpose is to make sure that the best product will be acquired to do the job at the least cost. To take an oversimplified example, assume choice between lighting a cigarette with a lighter or with a match. Which of the two methods is the most cost-effective, depends on whether you bought the matches or got them free, how much you paid for the lighter, how many lights you got from it, how expensive it is to operate, and how reliable.

The results of value analysis can be surprising. In the paper industry there is a disposable tool called a chipper blade that makes little chips out of big trees. For many years the industry used cheap domestic blades, until value analysis established that more expensive, imported blades had a longer life and therefore yielded more cuts per blade. This of course resulted in a lower cost of operation.

Standardization

It is important in purchasing to take full advantage of standardization. In this way it may be possible to realize quantity discounts or service benefits resulting from quantity buying. Where an industry has imposed uniformity of size and specification on its products regardless of manufacturer—the bearing industry, for example—deliberating between brands can be a waste of time and effort. A single brand should be chosen and adhered to without regard to subsequent efforts to impose personal preferences.

Effective Communication

Effective communication is essential to proper management of the purchasing function. Where there is no communication, there will be cases like that of the contractor whose auditor wrote an adverse report, criticizing a subcontractor for not buying against a centralized contract entered into by corporate headquarters. It turned out that the subcontractor had never been told of the buying contract's existence.

Some organizations seem to believe that there is nothing more to good communications than imposing purely formal documentary requirements. Collecting documents is a useless exercise unless specific information is sought. One company that buys $100 million in maintenance articles annually had a copy of each purchase order sent to headquarters in New York, where it was duly filed. Ultimately, the accumulation of copies filled 30 filing cabinets. When asked about this practice, the vice-president for purchasing explained that the benefits were basically psychological. "It's not what we do with the copies, it's what our people *think* we do with them." Actually not even this supposed benefit was being realized, because the home office was not questioning (and apparently never had questioned) the purchase orders. The whole elaborate procedure, which cost the company $160,000 annually (for stationery, postage, filing space, and filing cabinets), was a sham.

Adequate Lead Time

In the procurement and administrative processing of purchases, it is essential to allow adequate lead time, that is, a period between instructing the purchasing department and utilizing the materials. When materials are bought under pressure, their cost is likely to jump by up to 15 percent, an extra charge of which the buyer may not even be aware because it is usually not identified in the vendor's invoice. Even if there is no increase in unit cost, the failure to meet delivery schedules can result in construction delays which in turn may drastically elevate labor costs.

Expediting

One purchasing activity that frequently goes awry is expediting. Breakdowns in expediting are generally due to failure to assign responsibility for the activity among the various buyers—engineering, purchasing, and on-site—and subcontractors. The result of such breakdowns is that a certain percentage of items will not be available at the time they are supposed to be installed.

Advisability of Soliciting Bids

Purchasers are regularly faced with the decision of whether or not to seek bids. There are circumstances in which bid solicitation is pointless, for example where an item is made by only one company. The same may apply where commodities are subject to pricing as of the shipment date, as is the case with steel. If, however, there are significant differences between vendors in quality, service, or willingness to stock on the customer's behalf or to absorb the cost of certain services, bidding may still be advisable. If it should ever be necessary to waive bidding—as for example under emergency time pressures—the circumstances should be carefully documented so that they may be substantiated if necessary. Auditors now make it a practice to request such evidence, perhaps because so many cases of abuse of waiver have come to light. In one major American city, 30 percent of purchases are made under emergency conditions because of poor planning. The cost to the taxpayer is staggering.

Vendor Panel

An excellent method of dealing with vendors, especially subcontractors, is to set up a panel of those deemed eligible to receive bidding invitations. Members should be screened for financial stability, capacity to perform, backlog, and quality of supervision. All decisions relating to the bidding panel should be documented. If a purchasing agent inspects a contractor's facilities, he should keep a record of his visit. The eligibility of panelists should be reevaluated from time to time. If a panelist never bids or never receives an invitation to bid, little is to be gained by keeping him on the panel.

Bid Security

The processing of bids should be carried out under tight security. They should be received, unopened, by a supervisor who has no responsibility whatever for contract awards and should be dated and time stamped under that person's control. With large projects it is preferable that the bids be opened publicly.

There are other factors on which awards should be based besides price. The qualifications of the supervisors who would be assigned to the project are important. (The prime contractor should monitor the performance of these people throughout the life of the project.) Also important are equipment capabilities, backlogs, quality assurance procedures, and the provisions of union contracts.

If the project is large enough, it may be advisable to have bids for major contracts evaluated by an award committee composed of representatives of the engineering, purchasing, accounting, legal, and financial departments. The committee should be assigned to review the salient data, making certain that no bidder is eliminated without sufficient cause and that the most favorable contract terms are obtained. Where the amount of the award is very large, it might be desirable for the committee to submit its recommendations to management for the final decision.

Centralized Negotiations

A centralized buying department can contribute significantly to profitability by negotiating national buying contracts with companies having national distribution networks. In this way, price advantages are obtainable on a wide variety of goods, ranging from such items as valves and fractional horse-power motors to heating and lubricating oil. On one large project, the price negotiated on site was 15 percent higher than that in the national buying contracts. In a regional utility engaged in large scale construction, the centrally negotiated prices were exceeded substantially (by as much as 30 percent) at numerous sites. If local buyers can beat the national contract price at no sacrifice of quality, they should be free to do so. If, on the other hand, they buy at a higher price, the burden of justification rests on them.

CONTRACT ADMINISTRATION

Clear Terms

In negotiating contracts, it is important to use clearly defined terms, with full regard to the Uniform Commercial Code. It is also advisable to use standard terminology to enable negotiators to concentrate on the aspects that are not standard. Hard money contracts are desirable because they assure that any excess costs resulting from a subcontractor's inefficiency will be borne by him. However, this type of contract may be difficult to obtain, particularly if a project involves new technologies. Possible alternatives include granting awards on a temporary basis until detailed specifications become available, setting ceiling amounts above which costs will be further negotiated, and insistence on change-orders on a hard-money basis only.

One risk in operating under a letter of intent, rather than under a complete contract, is that the terms may differ from the owner's standard terms or may be vague or incomplete, resulting in differences of interpretation. For instance, a client negotiated a labor add-on percentage covering certain types of insurance and employee benefits. Since the work was proceeding under a letter of intent, however, there was no stipulation as to whether the add-on billing should be based on actual charges or whether it should be estimated, and, if so, whether the estimate should be adjusted to actual costs after the insurance company audit. The contractor, interpreting the clause in a manner favorable to himself, estimated the add-on. The resultant overcharge came to more than $1 million.

Where heavy equipment is involved, lease-versus-buy analyses must be made. Furthermore, if lease agreements are decided on, options to protect the right to purchase should be negotiated, where appropriate.

Expendable Items Defined

If the contracts call for extensive buying on the part of subcontractors, especially of small tools and minor equipment, establishment of ownership becomes an important consideration. For example, if a subcontractor is told to buy certain tools and return the unexpended ones when the job is finished, the word 'unexpended' must be defined precisely enough so that no misunderstandings will arise. One company that failed to do this found that of the $300,000 worth of articles it had deemed nonexpendable, the subcontractor returned or otherwise accounted for only $200,000. (Controls usually encompass perpetual records and a check-out and return system.)

Control of Change-Orders

Issuance and control of contract change-orders should be subject to procedures covering change-order initiation, approval, and processing. Change-orders should show estimated completion dates, man and equipment hours, and total cost. At times, questions may arise about whether work requested in change-orders is covered under existing contracts. It may, therefore, be advisable to mark disputed contract changes as made "under protest."

Effective Invoice Approval Routines

There should be appropriate accounting or physical controls for documents such as receiving reports or completion certifications, purchase orders or contract abstracts, and contractors' invoices. Clear lines of responsibility must be laid down for approval of invoices for payment. Generally, a percentage of the subcontractors' progress billings should be kept, but this practice should be supplemented by periodic timely reporting by construction supervisors on contractor performance.

Complete Purchase Order

Anyone working with purchase orders should be familiar with the following points. (They will be marked by italic type wherever mentioned.) *Freight terms* refers to the F.O.B. point at which title passes. Purchasing F.O.B. construction site makes it easier to compare prices and improve control over freight charges. If a purchase is made F.O.B. vendor's plant, the buyer normally has to absorb these charges. The seller may prepay the freight, collecting on delivery or rebilling the buyer. The party holding title is responsible for any damage in transit and normally for filing any claims that might be necessary. (From the point of view of good business practice, however, it might be worthwhile for the buyer to initiate the claim at the construction site, even if the vendor holds title.)

The choice of *freight routing* can have a significant effect on costs, particularly when heavy pieces are involved. The vendor is obviously going to select the route that is most advantageous to himself. Thus if he is near a railway siding, he might want to ship by rail even if another method would be better for the buyer. This is a negotiable point, however. If the same materials are habitually bought in the same cities, the freight cost could be made into an actual purchasing standard. Thus on all shipments of a particular item from say Detroit to New York, purchasing or traffic personnel would not be permitted to place orders whose freight costs would exceed a prescribed limit.

Under certain circumstances, the terms used on a purchase order to describe a material can determine whether it is taxable, and if it is taxable, whether the tax is deemed a sales or a use tax. For one thing, *sales taxes* may not be payable unless the recipient of the materials is also the end user. In addition, certain products bought for construction may be usable for other productive purposes, hence not taxable. There may also be advantages for the company in paying *use taxes* rather than sales taxes, especially where use taxes can be applied against tax deposits.

Quality specifications may have to be spelled out in the purchase order, particularly where highly complex or technical items are involved. In addition, if the order involves the type of material that must be vendor tested, that is that it cannot be subjected to the purchaser's ordinary incoming inspection (because of fragility, volatility, etc.), the purchase order should specify test documentation. (At times such items can only be tested on a batch basis, that is by using a number of samples taken from the same batch of materials.) The vendor should be obliged to supply a certification that all tests have been performed according to the purchaser's specifications and that the quality requirements have been met. Compliance should be checked at the time of delivery. If certification has not been demanded on the purchasing order and the tests have not been made, the purchaser could hardly expect to secure compliance at a later date.

Packing and delivery instructions should also appear on purchase orders. Many years ago, the Association of American Railroads substantially reduced the official weight for shipping cartons. Yet many materials are still shipped in unnecessarily heavy cartons, at additional freight expense. Whether items are to be shipped on pallets or in bags or are to be moved by air-handling equipment can affect costs. Unless definite directions are given, vendors can be expected to consult their own interest when it comes to details of packing, handling, and shipping, and the buyer may find himself with additional costs he had not reckoned on.

Systematic Contract Administration

Once contracts, including all amendments, modifications, and supplements have been negotiated, administrative procedures come into play. Central contract files should be maintained and abstracts of the contract prepared and distributed to all users of the information. This will prevent varying interpretations from arising between groups involved with the contract, such as the construction superintendents, the invoice approval clerks, and the internal auditors—a situation that would lead to mass confusion.

RECEIVING AND HANDLING MATERIALS

Qualitative Inspection

From the point of view of incoming inspection there are three classes of materials: those that cannot be inspected (see above, *Purchasing,* "Specifications"), those that involve special inspection procedures, and all others. For the most part, nuclear items fall into one of the first two categories; accordingly, it may be desirable to distinguish, on purchase orders or receiving reports, between nuclear and nonnuclear items. With respect to nuclear items, the special procedures are government-mandated inspection, tagging, and logging routines. If these controls are inefficiently applied, there is a good chance that the government will institute new procedures delaying work, and even withhold licensing.

Organizations that handle special-inspection items, especially nuclear items, should consider using the services of an internal quality assurance group that monitors inspections and assures that the government's standards are being complied with. Such groups should issue reports dealing with deficiencies and recommending corrective actions.

Quantitative Inspection

On large projects, where it would be uneconomic to weigh in every rail car or truck, statistical sampling of incoming loads can be employed to advantage. The weighing in of small parts may require the use of a logarithmic scale, which should be continuously checked for accuracy. The scale should be finely calibrated; surprisingly, many scales are deficient in this respect, even though it is well known that with logarithmic computation, the effect of errors is compounded.

It is customary for the seller to bear the costs of returning or—if repair is possible—of repairing defective materials. When there is a shortage, however, a question will arise as to who is responsible for the freight on the make-up shipment, unless the matter has been agreed on in advance.

As far as possible, all adjustments in connection with goods received should be initiated at the time of receipt—ideally before the shipment is accepted. (There is no better time to negotiate for overages, for example.) The responsibility for handling adjustment negotiations generally rests with the purchasing department acting on information transmitted to it by the receiving clerk. The receiving clerk's report, commonly termed the "Over, Short, and Damage Report," is thus of key importance. All claims and transactions connected with the disposition of claims should be carefully recorded.

Facilities Planning

The location and design of storage facilities involve detailed and careful planning based on an estimate of the total storage need and an analysis of the items to be stored. (Real and personal taxes may also be a consideration.) In general, the closer the storage facilities to the receiving area the lower the cost of moving materials. This consideration, however, must be balanced by the desirability of a central location from the point of view of distribution. The number of structures should be kept to a minimum. A single-structure arrangement has been found satisfactory even in large-scale projects. Under certain conditions, however, two structures, one centrally located and one near the edge of the construction area, may be desirable.

Storage buildings may be temporary or permanent. Builders often put up temporary structures without considering the possibility that the project owners might be able to use permanent buildings and might therefore be willing to defray much or even all of the extra cost involved.

Within the building, spatial arrangements should be carefully calculated to provide the best possible work flow. Given areas should be allocated to given categories of supplies and related items should be stored together. Each storage area should have sufficient space to serve as a buffer against overflow, which can clog movements and disrupt logical arrangements. At the same time, vacant space, whether inside or outside of the designated storage area, must be held to a minimum. Excessive space provides areas of escape from control and supervision; it can be used for caching stolen goods or just for goofing off. Storage facilities should be inspected frequently, not only to assure proper utilization of space, but also to remove temptation to requisition excessively. (The requisitioned items are often "squirreled away" in unauthorized storage areas.)

Also important is the selection of materials handling equipment. Inadequate crane capacity, for example, can lower efficiency by disrupting the flow of goods.

Because of the increasingly complex technology associated with construction, more and more companies are using professionals instead of day laborers to store and handle supplies. In any event, it might be a good idea to consider manning the senior positions with permanent employees who will become supply specialists, traveling from site to site and gaining a comprehensive knowledge of the stock.

Location

The location of materials in storage is indicated by locator records. These records are critical to the operation of the storage and supply facility. If they are not absolutely current, delays in filling requisitions are bound to occur and there will be a risk of a general breakdown in storage and supply. The best procedure for maintaining these records is to record storage location on the receiving document and then to post this information on a current basis to the locator record. When materials are transferred from one place to another, the accompanying documents must bear references to the locator records.

Inventory Records

Numbering schemes for storeroom articles can be important, especially when the storeroom system is automated. There are several technologically oriented numbering systems designed to establish a common language between construction crews, storekeepers, maintenance men, accountants, and others. Basically the systems employ two numbering setups. Articles used repetitively are grouped on a commodity basis, with subdivisions by nature, material, shape, and size; items used on specific machinery are coded with reference to the machine on which they are used.

To account for articles on hand, inventory records should be established. These do more than merely permit periodic comparisons of goods on hand to recorded quantities. They provide a guide to future planning of storage requirements, make it possible to detect slow inventory movement and minimize losses from obsolescence, and furnish the necessary information for timing reorders and for ordering in optimal quantities.

A system of written withdrawal requisitions is essential to proper accounting for inventory. The requirement for requisition should be applied with discrimination, however. To process an excessive number of requisitions for supplies of small value would be impractical. It is perfectly acceptable to make inexpensive items available on a self-service basis. Nuts and bolts, for example, can be dispensed from bins or from self-service trucks. Accounting entries need only be made when the dispensers are replenished.

Physical Controls

The requisition procedure can serve a control as well as a recordkeeping purpose. Thus, requiring the signature of a responsible authority whenever critical materials are involved curbs waste. Similarly, requiring borrowers to acknowledge in writing certain items deemed subject to pilferage will reduce losses from this source.

It may also be advisable to set up a "reverse requisitioning" system for returning articles to the supply department. Materials left at construction sites may be neglected or lost track of. In the case of items like copper cable, the cost of such waste could be high.

To minimize unnecessary recordkeeping, physical controls might be considered for inexpensive articles. With a physical system, the reorder-point stock is packaged separately. When that package is opened, the storeroom clerk detaches a reordering notice (similar to the type furnished with checkbooks) and forwards it to purchasing personnel. (Items critical to continuity of operations might have a safety-point package wrapped separately within the reorder-point package.)

Once inventory records have been instituted, periodic physical counts are necessary to preserve the records' accuracy. For the sake of economy, these counts (commonly termed "cycle counts" because the practice is to hold them at or near the reorder point) should be held on a late shift. It is important to test the accuracy of the counts and whether appropriate cutoff routines are in effect, and to segregate inventory adjustments for review. For larger contractors the cycle counting system should also be tested. If possible the testing should be done by the accounting department; it should not be done by storekeepers.

Slow movement of inventory poses the danger of obsolescence. To deal with the problem, a special committee (whose entire membership is not involved in the purchasing process) should be set up to review the problematic items and to make disposal recommendations. As a basis for these recommendations—which should of course be acted upon—the committee should prepare a preferential sequence of disposal options. Typically the order might be returned to the vendor (for credit less a handling charge), shipment to other projects, modification for eventual use, sale at a discount, and finally, scrapping. Where the committee deems disposal inadvisable, it should be prepared to support its decision with written evidence, such as statements by affected parties.

Control of Scrap Sales

Scrap quantities should be recorded at or near the point of generation. This helps to establish accountability and pinpoints scrap sources. It is of course desirable that scrap be sorted, especially as to type. Commingled scrap metals, for example, are generally paid for on the basis of the cheapest metal in the mixture. Sorting by size is also useful, but it can be carried to uneconomic extremes. To obtain the best prices for scrap metal, a company must be prepared to negotiate. Depending on the geographic location and on the nature and quantity of the metal, it may be possible to arrange competitive bidding. If so, this option should be weighed carefully against the advantages of striking bargains with individual scrap dealers. Of course, the persons in charge of scrap disposal should have a thorough knowledge of the market and of prevailing prices. In any case, dealer price quotations as well as weight reports should be checked for accuracy. If a company delivers its scrap to the dealers, it can save money by shipping in trailer loads rather than in carloads.

Storeroom Security

A systematic approach to storeroom security is essential. Access to the facilities should be via a limited number of entrances manned by guards in touch by telephone with the storeroom. All persons connected with the project should be required to wear identity badges whenever they are in the storeroom. (Some protection against employee pilferage is afforded by the requirement for written requisitions for withdrawal of certain items. See above, "Inventory Records.")Visitors should be asked to identify the storeroom person whom they are to see and should not be admitted until this party has acknowledged the expected visit. Logging of visitors in and out is advisable, and overlong visits should be viewed with suspicion. Spot inspections of outgoing vehicles are effective, but can produce ill-will. In general, it is not advisable to permit visitor or employee parking near the storage site.

LABOR AND EQUIPMENT

Productivity Measurement

In general, labor productivity is best measured by comparing actual performance with prepared standards. There are, for example, published data indicating how long a certain type of weld should take or how much labor is required to pour a yard of concrete. A simple technique that affords a gauge of labor productivity is the ratio delay study. This calls for observing large numbers of workers to determine the incidence of idleness. The results of these observations provide a starting point for evaluating the effectiveness of supervision.

In monitoring labor productivity, a contractor should consider not only his own employees but also those of the subcontractor. Too often, primary contractors ignore the productivity of subcontractor employees unless the contract calls for cost-plus. The reasoning is that with lump-sum contracts, labor efficiency is the subcontractor's headache. Changes in scope or timing, however, could turn a lump-sum contract into a cost-plus contract. Then, if labor performance has already been measured, the prime contractor has a much broader basis for reckoning payment than if measurement began only when the new contract went into effect. Furthermore, even when the contract remains lump-sum, production measurement can serve for reference in evaluating the subcontractor's overall performance.

Effective Timekeeping

The timekeeping function is of course essential to monitoring labor productivity. Thus timekeepers see to it that crews start, break, and quit at times specified in union contracts; they record absences and make sure that absentees are docked. (Some firms require craft personnel to wear specified hats, tags, or other identification to enable timekeepers to locate particular persons in particular scheduled activities.) Although principally concerned with craft workers, timekeepers may also extend their surveillance to the supervisory and administrative levels. Surprise on-site checks of staff personnel, for example, can supply data for evaluating the appropriateness of staff size. It is desirable that timekeepers not be drawn from the personnel of the locations at which they are functioning.

Minimization of Extra Shifts

In scheduling production, second and third shifts should be avoided insofar as possible. These shifts tend to be less productive because of the need to work under artificial lights (with lessened efficiency particularly evident in respect to set-up and tear-down time) and customarily "thin" timekeeping and supervisory routines (because of difficulties in getting white collar personnel to work on the off-shifts). In addition, many union contracts require a general wage boost whenever management institutes second and third shifts.

Control over Leased Equipment

Contractors who lease equipment should establish controls to make sure that they are getting what they paid for and are making good use of it. Where charges for equipment are based on condition, a careful inspection at the time of receipt is mandatory. (Such inspection is always advisable as protection against claims for misuse.) Subsequent inspections for condition are also advisable to record any deterioration in the equipment. The cost of the decreased efficiency resulting from deterioration could be made the basis for a rate adjustment, and in fact many leases so provide.

Another reason for inspection is to make sure that equipment is optimally employed. Idleness of equipment is costly and should be minimized by moving the equipment to where it is needed, whenever practicable.

Control must be established over cross billings to prevent double billing for equipment. This can happen when one subcontractor rents leased equipment to another subcontractor and both itemize their rental for the equipment as costs in their bills to the contractor.

The cost of maintaining and repairing leased equipment may be assumed by the lessee or by the lessor or may be apportioned between them according to some formula (which should be spelled out precisely in the contract). In practice, the actual responsibility for doing the work (or getting it done) together with the associated out-of-pocket costs, may fall to either party. Unless this party has assumed all repair and maintenance costs under the agreement, it must collect all or part of its out-of-pocket costs from the other party. Obviously careful recordkeeping is in order.

Bibliography

Adrian, James J. *CM: The Construction Management Process.* Reston, VA: Reston Publishing, 1981.

Ahuja, Hira N. *Construction Performance Control by Networks.* New York: Wiley, 1976.

Bean, Chester L. "Quality Can Be Maintained on Lump-Sum Construction." *Electrical World* (December 1982): 106-107.

Brickman, Bruce K. "Maintenance Clause Can Trip Users on Support." *Information Systems News* (January 24, 1983): 25-26.

Budwani, Ramesh N. "Power Plant Scheduling Construction, and Costs: 10-year Analysis." *Power Engineering* (August 1982): 36-49.

Diprima, Mike. "Engineering Change Control and Implementation Considerations." *Production and Inventory Management* (first quarter 1982): 81-82.

Harrington, Lisa H. "The Distribution Manager Takes on a Bigger Role." *Traffic Management* (December 1982): 37-40.

Hickok, Richard S. "New Guidance for Construction Contractors: A Credit Plus." *Journal of Accountancy* (March 1982): 44-54.

Kern, Dale R. "The Five W's of Construction Management." *Consulting Engineer* (January 1983): 48-52.

Kerzner, Harold. *Project Management for Executives.* New York: Van Nostrand Reinhold, 1982.

Kharbanda, O.P., Stallworthy, E.A., and Williams, L.F., (revised by James T. Stoms). *Project Cost Control in Action.* Englewood Cliffs, NJ: Prentice Hall, 1981.

"Management Contracts in Developing Countries: An Analysis of Their Substantive Provisions." *CTC Reporter* (Spring 1982): 17.

"More Construction for the Money: Summary Report of the Construction Industry Cost Effectiveness Project." *The Business Roundtable* (January 1983).

"More Equipment for Less Under New Leasing Rules." *Modern Materials Handling* (June 7, 1982): 63-65.

Muller, Frank. "The CE's Role in Construction Management." *Consulting Engineer* (January 1983): 53-57.

National Association of Women in Construction. *Construction Dictionary.* 5th ed. Greater Phoenix, Arizona Chapter #98, 1981.

Pomeranz, Felix. "Budgeting—Emerging Area of Audit Interest." *Journal of Accounting, Auditing and Finance* (Spring 1980): 270-275.

Pomeranz, Felix. "Control Construction Costs with Preemptive Auditing." *Power* (April 1983): 65–67.

Pomeranz, Felix. *Managing Construction Projects.* New York: Coopers & Lybrand, 1975.

Pomeranz, Felix. "Preemptive Auditing: Future Shock or Present Opportunity?" *Management Review* (August 1979): 18–21.

Pomeranz, Felix, and Gale, James. "Is This Strategy Working? A New Role for Accountants." *Management Review* (March 1980): 14–18.

"Professional Construction Management Services." The Subcommittee on Construction Management Organization and Evaluation, American Society of Civil Engineers. Convention exposition. Chicago October 16–20, 1978.

Quinn, Francis J. "Site Selection: Don't Take Anything for Granted." *Traffic Management* (December 1981): 53–56.

Sheldon, Robert G. "The Origin of the Ten Commandments of Production Control." *Production and Inventory Management Review* (April 1982): 16–18.

Stark, Norman, and Stark, C.D. *Construction Claims Investigation Worklist.* Professional Publications and Communications, Cleveland, OH, 1982.

Stein, J. Stewart. *Construction Glossary.* New York: Wiley, 1980.

Turner, W.S. III. *Project Auditing Methodology.* Amsterdam: North-Holland, 1980.

Ward, Sol A. and Litchfield, Thorndike. *Cost Control in Design and Construction.* New York: McGraw-Hill, 1980.

Index